This book belongs to

_____

DATE STARTED

The
DAUGHTER DETOX
Guided Journal
and
Workbook

A 7-STAGE PROCESS TO HELP
RECOVER FROM AN UNLOVING MOTHER

AND

RECLAIM YOUR SELF-ESTEEM

by **Peg Streep**

Designed & Illustrated by Claudia Karabaic Sargent

Île D'Éspoir Press

New York, New York

Published by Île d'Espoir Books, New York City

This book is designed to provide information and motivation to readers; the author is neither a therapist nor a psychologist. It is sold with the understanding that the author and publisher are not engaged to render any type of psychological or any other kind of professional advice. You should rely on the advice of your therapist or medical professional for decisions about your health, care, choices, and decisions; do not do any of the exercises in this book without consulting with him or her first. We strongly recommend that you follow the advice of your therapist or other professional when considering suggestions contained in the book. The author and publisher disclaim any liability for the use of this book. All of the names and identifying characteristics of people interviewed for this book have been changed and any similarity to any person is coincidental.

ISBN-13: 978-0692079553 (Custom Universal)
ISBN-10: 0692079556

This book was designed by Claudia Karabaic Sargent, and is typeset in the Bodoni URW font family, available through Adobe Typekit.

◈   ◈   ◈

TABLE OF CONTENTS

INTRODUCTION

Welcome, friends! *Bienvenue, mes amies!*

The book you're holding in your hands is the companion volume to *Daughter Detox: Recovering from an Unloving Mother and Reclaiming Your Life.* It's a special workbook and journal meant to make the exercises contained in the book easier, and it has lots of features that aren't a part of *Daughter Detox* itself. It's been created and designed by my longtime friend and collaborator, Claudia Karabaic Sargent, with uniquely designed coloring pages meant to inspire and support you. I've written the text.

The contents of *The Daughter Detox Journal* parallel the original book, helping you move through the stages that comprise the journey of recovery: **Discover, Discern, Distinguish, Disarm, Reclaim, Redirect,** and **Recover.** Because healing from the effects of a toxic childhood isn't a linear process, you may find yourself going back to earlier exercises and rereading even as you're trying to move forward; that's totally normal.

We've added Claudia's coloring pages—designed especially for you and your individual journey—because recent research shows that coloring is a calming activity for most adults as well as a creative way of expressing yourself. You can use crayons, colored pencils, or markers, but we recommend that you put a blank piece of white paper behind the page if you are using markers to prevent bleeding onto the following pages. The back of every coloring page is blank.

In addition to coloring, your journal has pages that ask you simply to think, question, and sometimes jot down a few words or catchphrases; pages with prompts for journaling to help you create a coherent narrative of your experience; and pages for visualization and other exercises and strategies to help you hone your emotional intelligence, reshape your ability to self-soothe and to deal with periods of stress and anxiety, and set new goals for yourself.

HOW THE JOURNAL IS ORGANIZED

The seven stages or steps described in my book *Daughter Detox: Recovering from an Unloving Mother and Reclaiming Your Life* give *The Daughter Detox Journal* its shape. Following is a brief summary of those stages, drawn from the original book, which describe the journey of the unloved daughter from pain and influence to freedom and choice.

Discover: Many daughters emerge into adulthood without knowing the extent to which they have been wounded in childhood, how their mothers' treatment of them has shaped their behaviors, and how much of their present unhappiness and distress is actually a function of childhood experiences. It sounds counterintuitive but it's true, so that the first step is actually discovering what happened to you in childhood. There are many reasons discovery is necessary, all of them explained in the book, but they include a daughter's denial of her treatment, her *"normalizing"* what she experienced in her family of origin, and her continuing need for her mother's love and attention. This stage also includes figuring out your own attachment style: do you display patterns of secure attachment or one of the three types of insecure attachment?

Discern: These pages focus on coming to terms with and understanding the relational patterns in your childhood home and how your own behaviors, thoughts, and feelings were a response to your treatment by others, including your father. Most important, this includes beginning to see the behaviors that trigger your responses and the coping mechanisms you developed in childhood and how they impact your present.

Distinguish: This section is devoted to helping you see how the relational patterns from the past persist into the present, and how they affect how happy you are today and whether you're able to thrive in healthy, sustaining relationships. The specific exercises and questions are aimed at having you look below the surface and examine your closest relationships and your own motivations.

Disarm: The goal of this part of the journal is to help you battle those triggers—the unconscious impulses to choose the wrong people for friendship, partnership, and love because they treat you in ways that echo your childhood experiences, or those that evoke outsized and potentially self-defeating behaviors—and to replace them with different impulses and conscious thinking and decision-making. This part of the journal picks up the pace in terms of intensity, delving into your thoughts and feelings, having you work on increasing your emotional intelligence and curbing your reactivity.

Reclaim: The theme of this section is taking back your power. This stage is the first step to setting new goals and rerouting your life through journaling and other exercises that examine how you deal with challenges and stress and help you cope in more productive ways. Stopping ruminative habits of thought, learning how to reframe experiences and implement *"if/then"* thinking, and using visualization are all discussed and explained.

Redirect: With newfound self-knowledge, the question becomes *"What choices do I need to make to live a happier, more content life?"* Resolving old conflicts, including how to handle your relationships to your mother and other family members, is the focus here, with the emphasis on clarifying your thinking, labeling and identifying your feelings with more precision, and helping detangle conflicting emotions. The needs to increase your self-compassion and learn to mother yourself are addressed with specific steps to take.

Recover: The book on which this journal is based embraces a different vision of what it means to heal from childhood experience. This stage explores and explains the Japanese art of *kintsugi* and how to apply its vision to your life going forward. This ancient process of repairing broken or damaged objects deliberately highlights the fissures and cracks with gold or silver joinery, making its woundedness part of its beauty. This vision of what it means to make something "whole" runs counter to Western thinking where we understand making something whole as equivalent to making it look as though nothing ever happened to it. Exercises and special journal prompts in this last section will help you move forward into the future with a new vision of healing.

ABOUT JOURNALING AND PROMPTS

The work of James Pennebaker and others has shown that writing helps us make sense of our experiences and permits us to connect the dots—seeing cause and effect—that simply thinking about events and interactions in our lives doesn't. Creating a coherent narrative of our lives allows us to see our lives and experiences with a new perspective. Many people freeze when they see the blank pages of traditional journals, which is why, after hearing from many of you, we decided a format with prompts and rules would remove a significant obstacle for many. There's no hard and fast rule on how to use the prompts; you can use them as inspiration and take off from them or respond literally. Try if you can to answer in full sentences. If the prompt is a question, pretend that you're in a conversation.

Please keep in mind that journaling isn't a test of your writing ability or articulateness. No one cares how well you spell or whether your grammar is impeccable. No one is asking you to be a poet either. This project is an effort to help you think hard about things that are hard to think about and to help you make sense of what's happened in your life. The closer you get to putting your previously unexamined thoughts into words on the page, the better the journal will work for you.

There's a fair amount of emotional confusion that's a common legacy of a childhood dominated by an unloving mother, and journaling absolutely can help, provided you pay attention to one key rule: *using cool processing.*

Recalling what we felt at a distressing or hurtful time in our lives can actually act as a trigger and have us feel the pain of the experience as though it were happening again. That can be harmful to you in many ways, especially if you experienced abusive behaviors growing up. It's very important that you learn to focus not on what you felt but why you felt it. That is the essence of cool processing.

HOW TO COOL-PROCESS

When you pull up a memory, you need to do it from a specific perspective—that of a third party or a stranger who sees it from a distance. So we'd like you to take the stance of an observer, seeing your experience for the first time at a great remove. Imagine seeing what happened in your childhood living room as a stranger might see it, standing on a hilltop.

Now focus on **why** you felt as you did so that you can begin to see how your emotions are responses in context and how your thoughts were formed in response to things said and done. Let's say, for example, that you are recalling watching your mother argue with your father as a child. Rather than focus on **what** you felt (*"I was really scared and shaking because my father was yelling that he was going to leave her forever"*), instead you would think about **why** you felt as you did: *"My parents' fights made life at home seem so precarious. Every time they fought, I'd worry about being abandoned by both of them or, even worse, being left alone with my mother without my dad's protection. I still get afraid when anyone yells."*

Cool processing is a learned skill and you should take your time practicing it if it's new to you. Please pay close attention to your feelings and at the first sign of hot processing—you're recalling what you felt and reliving it—STOP. Shut the journal and calm yourself. This is a hard and fast rule for using this book and you must take it seriously.

THIS JOURNAL IS A COMPANION TO THE BOOK

While you don't have to be reading the book as you fill in the journal, the journal hasn't been designed as a stand-alone either. The exercises and journal pages are designed to amplify the takeaway lessons of the original text.

We *do* suggest that you work the sections in order, beginning with *Discover,* although we expect you to go back to earlier sections as you move forward as described in the following pages.

WHAT YOU SHOULD DO BEFORE YOU START *THE DAUGHTER DETOX JOURNAL*

Choose a place in your home where you will do the work this book entails. Science shows that humans are unconsciously influenced by their surroundings so it's important that you think about where you want to work. Don't pick a place that will distract you by making you think of all the things you should be doing; journaling while your eye rests on a sink full of dirty dishes is counterproductive. Do choose a place where you feel comfortable and where you can work relatively undisturbed. It's a good idea to do your journaling and exercises in the same place every time.

It may be helpful to you to choose some objects that have emotional meaning or images that make you feel calm when you look at them and bring them into the area you've chosen. You may also want to light a scented candle as you work, or have some flowers nearby. Photographs of people who matter in your life can also make you feel more grounded. If you are calmed by music and are able to have it playing in the background without being distracted, go right ahead.

Choose a time to work on the journal when you won't be interrupted or distracted by checking the clock or feeling rushed. Parts of the journal require you to do some deep thinking and you'll want to do this thoroughly and calmly. Don't start a section when you know you have to run out or when you're expecting a phone call. Commitment to the process actually matters when you're battling old habits of mind.

Listen to your body. In the best of all possible worlds, you'll be working on the journal when you feel calm, relatively relaxed, and up to the task of confronting the past. It may be best for you to calm yourself before you start by visualizing someone you love and feel safe with or a place that makes you feel happy and relaxed; studies show that this really works! If a question or a prompt makes you anxious or you feel your throat tighten or have some other physical reaction, please **stop**. There'll be another time to do the work.

USING THE JOURNAL

Please keep in mind that the wounds you suffered in childhood took a long time to inflict and involve literally hundreds, if not thousands, of interactions and experiences. It's not surprising, then, that healing is a long and slow process. There is, alas, no magic wand to "fix" things right up. Neither this journal nor the book on which it's based promise a quick fix either. Because I'm neither a therapist nor a psychologist, all the exercises are suggested by research findings. When there's a thinking exercise, feel free to grab a piece of paper to jot down notes if you feel that will be of help to you. In fact, you can adapt or add to any of the journaling exercises by using separate pieces of paper.

All of the exercises, including journaling, require **cool processing** and are meant to help you begin to think about and make sense of your childhood experiences (and some of your present ones) without releasing an emotional cascade or making you anxious.

The goal of the journal is to help you get on a path of self-knowledge so that you're able to lessen and ultimately be free of the negative influence of the past. This book, like the one on which it's based, is **not** a substitute for therapy. If you are currently in therapy, please discuss your use of this book with your counselor. Therapy is a proven way of dealing with the emotional and psychological fallout from childhood experiences.

USING THE EXERCISE INDEX

In order to build a particular skill set—using visualizations or labeling emotions, for example—you may find it useful to do certain exercises more than once, and do all the related ones in sequence. To that end, we've provided an index, organized by subject matter, on page 200 to make it easier for you.

REDEFINING PROGRESS AS TWO STEPS FORWARD, ONE STEP BACK

I'm neither a psychologist nor a therapist but I have walked this path myself and have spent the better part of 15 years researching and listening to other unloved daughters. We like thinking of progress as a steady climb up a hill but when it comes to this kind of recovery, it's really not. The best analogy I can come up with is to visualize a game of pick-up sticks, and the sticks stand for your thoughts, emotions, and behaviors. When you play the game, sometimes you pick up a stick that shows you a clear path to getting the others without any other stick moving but, sometimes, when you pick up one, it just creates another jumble. That's true of recovery, too. This journal has been designed with that in mind with back-and-forth between the sections for that very reason.

WHAT NOT TO DO WHEN USING THIS BOOK

Start ruminating

Get obsessive

Second-guess your memories

Feel guilty

Think you're the only one (because you're not)

WHAT TO DO WHEN USING THIS BOOK

Practice self-compassion

Cut yourself some slack

Praise yourself on progress made

Remind yourself you're lovable

Focus on the future

To get in touch with me, go to *www.pegstreep.com*
or *www.facebook.com/PegStreepAuthor*

GODSPEED!
Peg Streep

DISCOVER

One of the paradoxes about this journey is that many daughters don't see or identify either their emotional wounds or the source of them. They've either normalized their treatment in childhood or denied the pain or made excuses for their treatment because they still need their mothers' love and support. That's why discovery of how your past affects your present is the first step.

Bringing the unconscious into consciousness is hard work so we'll proceed slowly. In the best of all possible worlds, you'll do these exercises over the course of days rather than all at once. When you're doing the thinking exercises, consider them an opportunity to explore your inner thoughts and feelings, pulling what's remained unarticulated to the surface. The goal is for you to gain clarity about your thoughts, possible conflicts within you that you might not be conscious of, and for you to accrue valuable self-knowledge that has previously been out of reach.

Understanding the power your mother had to shape how you saw the world and the people in it, realizing how her vision of you became the template for how you saw yourself, and grasping how that early understanding still influences you today are key parts of the process. Becoming aware of the core conflict in you—the growing recognition of how you were treated and how you adapted in ways that don't serve you coexists absolutely with your continuing need for maternal love and support—is another aspect of this part of the journey.

Recognizing the power mothers have over their children and understanding that the power can be abused run counter to all the myths about motherhood our culture holds dear. Grasping the truth about your life can make you feel more isolated and more like an outsider, but be assured that that's not true. While there are many daughters with loving mothers, just slightly less than half of us didn't get our emotional needs met in childhood.

IDENTIFYING YOUR ATTACHMENT STYLE

Thinking Exercise #1

Which attachment style best describes you?

Remember that these distinctions are not carved in stone and that you are trying to figure out how you react most of the time.

Secure attachment: You feel good about yourself and the choices you make and you feel confident about your ability to know what you're thinking and feeling most of the time. You value relationships in all their forms and are confident that you have the ability to choose partners and friends wisely. You tend not to second-guess yourself or worry about choices you make most of the time.

Anxious/Preoccupied: You worry constantly about relationships and are always on the lookout for things going wrong or signs that the person you're with, whether it's a friend or a lover, is either about to decamp or lying to you. You take umbrage at gestures you consider slights, and are very jealous. You have to restrain yourself not to peek at his email or texts. You have an argumentative style when there's relational stress.

Avoidant/Dismissive: Do you tend to think that other people are just too needy and not independent enough? Do you feel you're really above the fray and self-reliant? You have a generally high opinion of yourself and your competence but not of others. Confiding in others just isn't your thing and you are content to go it alone.

Avoidant/Fearful: Do you tend to see people generally as untrustworthy and unreliable and do you shy away from any relationship that would really make you feel vulnerable and susceptible to being hurt? Or are you always quick to focus on why the person you're with isn't right for you, how his or her flaws make getting along impossible? You don't feel especially secure in yourself but, then again, you don't feel secure in the company of others either.

Catchphrase Exercise #1

The point of this exercise is for you to write down words or phrases that best describe you when you're in a relationship and how you behave. The goal here is for you to begin to see how your attachment style affects you in all different kinds of relationships, from the casual acquaintance to a coworker or colleague to a close friend or a lover. Try to make your thinking as free-flow as possible.

Here are some possible examples:

> *Jump to conclusions*   *Worry constantly*   *Try hard to please*
> *Turn off quickly*   *Nervous and watchful*   *Open and willing*
> *Calm and thoughtful*   *Armored and hesitant*

_____   _____

_____   _____

_____   _____

_____   _____

_____   _____

❖   ❖   ❖

Thinking Exercise #2

Focus on a relationship you're in or that you were in recently; it should be a relationship that was more than casual, in which you felt you really got to know the other person. Think about that person's attachment style and how it affected the dynamic of your connection. Was this a relationship in which one person was the Giver, the other the Taker, or was there a mutual give-and-take? Reflecting on this person, do you think he or she is largely secure in his or her attachment style, anxious/preoccupied, or avoidant? If it's the latter, think about which kind of avoidant: dismissive or fearful. Finally, think about what attracted you to this person in the first place or, if the relationship is ongoing, continues to attract you.

❖   ❖   ❖

Catchphrase Exercise #2

Describe the person's character and behaviors in a free-flow manner in a series of words or phrases. Some examples are:

Introverted but thoughtful   *Outgoing and easygoing*

Hard to draw out   *Preoccupied and distant*

Smart   *Witty*   *Self-involved*

_____   _____

_____   _____

_____   _____

_____   _____

Catchphrase Exercise #3

Describe the dynamic in the relationship as fully as you can, using the two-column format so that one column describes you and the other, your partner. See the example following for how to do this.

Geri	*Eliot*
anxious/preoccupied	secure
argumentative	peacemaker
outgoing and active	introvert, but willing to compromise
sloppy, goes with the flow	neat freak, careful
grudge-holding	talks things through, forgives

_____ _____

_____ _____

_____ _____

_____ _____

_____ _____

◈　◈　◈

IDENTIFYING YOUR MOTIVATIONS

Thinking Exercise #3

Are you generally more motivated by approach or avoidance? Say you've been offered an opportunity at work. Are you more likely to take it—even if there's a chance you might fail utterly at it—or, when you start thinking about it, is all you can focus on how you'd feel if you failed? Similarly, if you're in a relationship that's going through a rough patch, are you more likely to initiate a discussion, no matter how difficult, that might fix the problems you're having or are you more likely to avoid talking about it directly and let sleeping dogs lie? Generally, are you more focused on taking risks in the hopes of succeeding or are you homed in on making as few mistakes in life as possible?

Thinking Exercise #4

If you're largely a *"go for it no matter what"* person, think about the childhood experiences you had that helped you become that way. Think about how your mother's point of view affected your willingness to take chances. Alternatively, if you're always focused on not making a mistake and you tend to avoid situations at which you might fail, what do you think made you worry about failing? Think about the role your mother played in how you looked at and still evaluate challenges.

Journaling Exercise #1

Understanding how you handle stress and challenges as a result of your childhood experiences is an important component of recovery since the chances are good that you're not reaching your full potential in some areas of life. Increased self-knowledge won't just make you happier; it will also allow you to go in new directions with more confidence. Spend some time looking at the prompts, allowing your true thoughts to float to the surface. Then write. The first series of prompts are statements and the second series is comprised of questions for you to answer.

As a girl, the idea of failing made me feel _____

_____

_____

_____

_____

My family's definition of success was _____

_____

_____

_____

My mother pressured me to _____

_____

_____

_____

_____

As an adult, personal challenges make me feel _____

_____

_____

_____

_____

I react to stress and challenges by _____

_____

_____

_____

_____

I deal with setbacks by _____

_____

_____

_____

_____

During your childhood, what did your mother say about your achievements? _____

_____

_____

_____

_____

_____

Growing up, did a challenge or competition inspire or threaten you? _____

_____

_____

_____

_____

How did you handle failure as a child? _____

_____

_____

_____

_____

How often do you second-guess yourself and your decisions? _____

_____

_____

_____

_____

Are you prone to feeling regret about your choices? _____

_____

_____

_____

_____

How confident are you? _____

_____

_____

What qualities in yourself hold you back most? _____

_____

_____

_____

_____

_____

_____

Do you consider yourself successful? If yes, why? If not, why? _____

_____

_____

_____

_____

_____

Is other people's opinion of you important? Why? _____

_____

_____

_____

_____

_____

PROCESSING MEMORIES

**DO NOT WRITE ANYTHING DOWN AND,
IF YOU ARE FEELING ANXIOUS,
SIMPLY STOP IMMEDIATELY.
YOU MUST USE COOL PROCESS.**

Thinking Exercise #5

Begin to cool-process by recalling a specific incident either from your childhood or any other point in your life that involves your interacting with your mother. Again: Do not relive the moment in a blow-by-blow way because that will just have you reexperience your feelings and won't do anything to increase your understanding. Recall the incident as though you are seeing it from a distance and as though it happened to someone else. Focus on why you felt as you did. What do you see now in the pattern of interaction that you might not have before?

Following are examples of hot and cool processing drawn from my own life.

Hot-process recall:

I'm six or so and I'm in the schoolyard on the jungle gym. A boy pushes me off and I land hard on the ground. There is so much blood pouring out of my head, and my legs are bloody. I'm scared and crying and I want my mommy. I am waiting in the nurse's office and my mother comes in. She doesn't hug me but says, "What did you do now? Don't get close; I don't want blood on my silk blouse." The nurse explains but the minute we get out of the building, my mother starts yelling at me about her missed hairdresser's appointment and how now she has to take me to the doctor, which makes me cry harder. My nose is dripping because I am crying so hard. I remember how scared I was and how I wanted to be cuddled, and how much my head hurt. I am shaking thinking about her cruelty. Her yelling in the car and then at home. She was angry because I ruined her day. It's all painful to remember.

Cool-process recall:

I fell from the jungle gym at school when I was six because a boy pushed me. My head was bleeding like crazy and the teacher swooped me up and ran to the nurse with me and called my mother. I was scared and crying because there was so much blood. My mother came to get me and she was enormously angry because now she had to take me to the doctor instead of going to the hairdresser. She didn't hug me or kiss me. She yelled at me all afternoon, and into the evening. I remember how scared I was and hurt that she wouldn't hug me but I also remember being angry. I knew I wasn't being treated right. I just didn't know how to put it into words.

Journaling Exercise #2

Go back to the interaction you focused on in Thinking Exercise #5 on page 23 and write about it using cool processing and the benefit of hindsight, and then answer the questions that follow.

_____

_____

_____

_____

_____

_____

_____

_____

_____

◈   ◈   ◈

What typical patterns in your family of origin does this encounter reveal?

_____

_____

_____

_____

Using hindsight, what can you now say about your mother's behavior?

_____

_____

_____

_____

What insight do you have now that you didn't when the interaction took place?

_____

_____

_____

_____

What would you say to your younger self about this moment?

_____

_____

_____

_____

How is your adult self shaped by this and other moments like it?

_____

_____

_____

_____

What have you learned from retrieving and cool-processing this memory?

_____

_____

_____

_____

THE MATERNAL PATTERNS

Thinking Exercise #6

Of the eight toxic patterns—*dismissive, controlling, unavailable, unreliable, self-involved, combative, enmeshed, role-reversed*—which most accurately describes how your mother treated you most of the time in childhood and adolescence? Most unloving mothers display more than one type of behavior; for example, a mother who is dismissive of a young daughter may become controlling as the child gets older. Think about her behaviors in detail, thus preparing yourself for the next catchphrase exercise.

Catchphrase Exercise #4

Using cool recall, write down the behaviors (dismissive, controlling, etc.) that best characterized your mother when you were young. Then, in the spaces below, enter the catchphrases drawn from memory. Here is an example of one:

Dismissive

Pretended she didn't hear me or that I didn't say what I'd said

Mocked and laughed at me or called me names

Always said other people—even friends I brought home—were better than I was

If I did something good, she said it didn't matter

Used food to manipulate me, make me feel bad, told me I was fat

Told me no one would ever like me, love me

Said my friends were using me

Encouraged my siblings to gang up on me

_____

_____

_____

_____

_____

_____

_____

_____

_____

_____

_____

_____

_____

_____

◈   ◈   ◈

Journaling Exercise #3

Recall an incident from your childhood, recent past, or even present that involved an interaction with your mother. Do what you can to recall the time and place, and how old you were at the time. Report what you said and did, what she said and did, without detail—just the barest of bones and free of emotion. Now shift your focus to why you felt as you did. *("I felt as though nothing I said mattered because her face turned to stone and she didn't even bother answering me" or "She turned her back on me when I started talking and walked away, and I felt as if she'd waved a wand and disappeared me.")*

If you are beginning to cry or feeling your muscles tighten, you need to practice cool processing more before writing. That's to be expected; this exercise tests your ability to manage your emotions and that's exactly what most of us aren't very good at.

What sparked the moment or interaction? _____

_____

_____

_____

_____

_____

Where the exchange took place, who was present, and how old you were _____

_____

_____

_____

_____

What was said by whom _____

_____

_____

_____

_____

If someone else was present, please describe his or her reaction _____

_____

_____

_____

_____

_____

How it made you feel _____

_____

_____

_____

_____

_____

Did you spend time thinking about what happened? Why? _____

_____

_____

_____

_____

Why is this particular memory important or symbolic? _____

_____

_____

_____

_____

In retrospect, do you see something in the exchange that you didn't at the time?

_____

_____

_____

_____

If you confronted your mother and asked to discuss this moment, what would she say?

_____

_____

_____

_____

_____

WORKING ON BOUNDARIES

Thinking/Catchphrase Exercise #7

Boundaries are an issue for unloved daughters; despite their styles of engagement, all of these mothers disregard them, if in different ways. Recognizing boundaries—those invisible lines between the person that's you and the person that is the other—is part and parcel of maintaining healthy relationships that permit deep connection and emotional support and, at the same time, still leave your self complete without feeling subsumed, taken over, or hijacked.

What bothers you more? Intrusiveness or exclusiveness? Having someone nose to nose or someone who's shut you out? Use the following spaces to write down catchphrases about boundaries.

_____   _____

_____   _____

_____   _____

_____   _____

_____   _____

Journaling Exercise #4

Recall a recent incident with another person that involved boundaries or the absence of them. This could be about your mother, a family member, a friend, or anyone you would like to write about.

Describe the incident _____

_____

_____

_____

_____

_____

What was the boundary issue? _____

_____

_____

_____

_____

In what way did you contribute to the problem? _____

_____

_____

_____

_____

In what way did the other person contribute? _____

_____

_____

_____

_____

What does this tell you about your ability to successfully navigate and negotiate boundaries? _____

_____

_____

_____

_____

LOOKING AT YOURSELF

Journaling Exercise #5

Pretend that you are a friend talking about you. It could be a woman or a man. Follow the prompts and write free-flow, without censoring yourself. If you find this exercise too difficult to do at this point, skip it and you can go back to it.

❖   ❖   ❖

The first thing you notice about her is _____

_____

_____

_____

_____

The second thing you see is _____

_____

_____

_____

_____

What I like best about her is _____

_____

_____

_____

_____

_____

What it's like spending time with her: _____

_____

_____

_____

Her best qualities and strengths are _____

_____

_____

_____

_____

Her weaknesses include _____

_____

_____

_____

_____

What, if anything, you'd change about her _____

_____

_____

_____

_____

Journaling Exercise #6

Out of the following list of words, pick those that best describe how you see yourself. Then write a sentence or two about each word and how and why it describes you accurately.

outgoing	withdrawn	sincere	obsessive	guarded
introverted	high-strung	nervous	focused	weak
funny	easygoing	smart	open	shy
sensitive	strong-willed	stubborn	confident	voluble
overly sensitive	hardworking	hardnosed	quiet	impulsive
anxious	reactive	reserved	boring	snooty
creative	extraverted	dull	suspicious	armored
manipulative	resilient	cautious	careful	witty
persistent	articulate	strong	critical	tough

_____

_____

_____

_____

_____

_____

_____

_____

_____

_____

_____

_____

_____

_____

_____

_____

_____

_____

_____

_____

_____

_____

_____

_____

_____

_____

_____

_____

_____

_____

DISCERN

Once you have begun to see and discover the roots of your inner unease, the task at hand is to build your conscious awareness by discerning the patterns of relationship in your family of origin, what coping mechanisms you developed, and how the roles people played shaped your emotional and psychological development.

Bringing these patterns to light requires you to focus on the family's dynamics, the role your father played in his absence or presence, and your relationships to your siblings if you had them. This perspective will allow you to see your reactions and responses in context. This is especially true if your mother treated you differently from your siblings or if you were singled out in specific ways. If you were an only child, that needs to be looked at with care.

Next, you'll take an unflinching look at your mother's treatment of you, both in the past and in the present, and home in on how her behaviors influenced not just your sense of yourself and your abilities but also how you approach relationships, how you behave in times of stress, and how able you are to manage your emotions and thoughts. Coming to terms with how many of your behaviors in the present are animated and driven by the experiences of the past, particularly your interactions with your mother, is key to the process of healing. Since most of our ways of connecting to others are driven by unconscious processes, discerning those processes is an important and sometimes challenging task.

By bringing what's hidden into the light, you can begin to take ownership of your past and start to take command of your future.

SEEING THE HOUSEHOLD

Thinking Exercise #8

Using cool processing, recall an incident from your childhood that captures what it was like to grow up in your household. Focus specifically on the behaviors of each family member.

Catchphrase Exercise #5

Under each column, write down—using off-the-top-of-your-head thinking—what comes to mind about each of your family members, including yourself. If you have more siblings, please use an extra piece of paper. If you were an only child, use the space to describe how you felt most of the time, using catchphrases. In addition to focusing on personality and proclivities, you may want to use some of the words listed below:

dominant	*domineering*	*submissive*
secure	*insecure*	*enabling*
bullying	*supportive*	*detached*
engaged	*weak*	*strong*
obedient	*rebellious*	*complacent*

<u>Mother</u>

_____   _____   _____

_____   _____   _____

_____   _____   _____

<u>Father</u>

_____   _____   _____

_____   _____   _____

_____   _____   _____

<u>Me</u>

_____   _____   _____

_____   _____   _____

_____   _____   _____

Sibling #1

_____ _____ _____

_____ _____ _____

_____ _____ _____

Sibling #2

_____ _____ _____

_____ _____ _____

_____ _____ _____

◈   ◈   ◈

Journaling Exercise #7

The goal of this exercise is for you to bring new clarity and understanding to the behaviors and motivations of those who made up your childhood world. Spend some time thinking before you answer.

Was there a dominant parent? Who was it and how did he or she wield power?

_____

_____

_____

_____

_____

Describe the relationship between your parents as you saw it as a child. _____

_____

_____

_____

_____

Describe their relationship as you understand it as an adult.

_____

_____

_____

_____

Was the household openly argumentative or were behaviors covert? Please describe.

_____

_____

_____

_____

Did your mother treat her children differently? Please describe. _____

_____

_____

_____

_____

When you were a child, how did you make sense of how she treated your siblings?

_____

_____

_____

_____

As a kid, did you think your household was normal or somehow different? Explain.

_____

_____

_____

_____

_____

◇　　◇　　◇

Journaling Exercise #8

Using cool processing, please write about the incident or event you recalled and thought about in Thinking Exercise #8, page 40. As you write, describe the dynamic and interactions of the personalities in the household with as much detail and accuracy as you can and analyze why this one moment is typical.

_____

_____

_____

_____

_____

_____

_____

_____

_____

_____

_____

THE EXTENDED FAMILY AND BEYOND

Were there relatives, neighbors, family friends, teachers, mentors, or other adults who played a role as an influencer in your childhood? It might have been a grandmother or grandfather, an aunt, or even your Sunday school teacher or someone else?

Seeing how these people beyond the immediate family contributed to your childhood experiences—either by offering you safe shelter and an alternative reflection of yourself or helping bolster the family line about you, or a mix of both—will help you take another, broader look at how you and your behaviors were shaped in childhood.

In the spaces below, name the person and describe the role he or she played in your childhood and how the connection affected your sense of self.

_____

_____

_____

_____

_____

_____

_____

_____

_____

_____

_____

_____

_____

_____

_____

Journaling Exercise #9

This is a series of emotional intelligence workouts to help you label and identify your feelings with more clarity and accuracy. Study the list below before you begin, and circle the words that apply to you. Feel free to add in words that aren't listed in the blank slots.

upset	*fractious*	*sad*
disconnected	*tense*	*depressed*
afraid	*on edge*	*relaxed*
angry	*alone*	*empty*
tense	*isolated*	*numb*
bewildered	*belligerent*	*walled off*
anxious	*worried*	*armored*
happy	*hopeful*	*watchful*
secure	*hopeless*	*calm*
uncomfortable	*defensive*	*adrift*
hurt	*cautious*	*neutral*
self-reliant	*needy*	*strong*
insecure	*confused*	*clear*
worthy	*unworthy*	*cynical*
disappointed	*buoyed*	*optimistic*
detached	*engaged*	*weak*
overcome	*obedient*	*rebellious*
demeaned	*dismissed*	*diminished*
bullied	*scapegoated*	*gaslighted*

_____ _____ _____

_____ _____ _____

_____ _____ _____

Using the list of words above, write the following descriptions. Try to aim at capturing the complexity of your emotions. Do this in full sentences.

How you felt when you were alone with your mother as a child _____

_____

_____

_____

_____

_____

How you felt when you were alone with your mother as an adolescent _____

_____

_____

_____

_____

How you felt when you were alone with your father growing up _____

_____

_____

_____

_____

How you felt when the family was gathered together _____

_____

_____

_____

_____

Thinking Exercise #9

Fathers influence their daughters' development in significant ways, both by what they do and say, and what they don't. You can use the following descriptions of the roles fathers play from *Daughter Detox* to guide your thinking if you wish. Focus in on your father's behaviors and how they shaped your sense of yourself.

The Yes Man: Devoted to and inseparable from Team Mom, either because he's chosen sides or because he's an Appeaser and just wants something that is a poor imitation of peace.

The Chorus: Fathers can be emotionally abusive and withheld, too, and some daughters are doubly unlucky to have two parents who are alike in this way, though their behaviors may be different.

The King of the Castle: You want and need your father's attention but your mother considers you a threat to her dominance, and your efforts to get close to him only amp up her jealousy and abusive treatment of you.

The Absentee: This father isn't present either metaphorically (hides in his study or behind a newspaper, pretends nothing is going on, or withdraws from the fray) or is literally absent from the household.

The Rescuer: While he doesn't actively debate his wife's treatment of you, he does negotiate a tricky terrain and is a source of caring, advice, and support for you.

Journaling Exercise #10

Using cool recall, describe an event or encounter with your father that captures the essence of your relationship. Focus on why you were feeling as you did and describe those emotions in detail.

_____

_____

_____

_____

_____

_____

_____

_____

_____

_____

◈   ◈   ◈

Thinking Exercise #10

Sibling relations are a complicated affair. Spend time reflecting on your relationship to your sibling or siblings, and how the presence of each changed how you saw yourself in both positive and negative ways. If you are an only child, please reflect on the pluses and minuses connected to being a singleton and how they influenced your growth.

◈   ◈   ◈

Journaling Exercise #11

Answer the following questions, spending more time thinking and reflecting on your answers than writing. If you are an only child, go to the questions below marked *"singletons"*. For those who have a sibling who is seven years younger or more (meaning you spent a large part of childhood as an only), you might want to answer the singleton questions as well.

To what degree did your mother orchestrate or meddle in sibling relationships? Describe as

accurately as you can. _____

_____

_____

_____

_____

_____

Did your siblings see your mother as you did in childhood? Describe the effect their views had on you. _____

_____

_____

_____

_____

Describe how your sibling relationships affect you in adulthood. _____

_____

_____

_____

_____

How do these relationships complicate or ameliorate your relationship to your mother?

_____

_____

_____

_____

For singletons:
What do you consider is the most profound effect of being an only child?

_____

_____

_____

_____

In what ways is your relationship to both parents complicated by being an only child?

_____

_____

_____

_____

_____

Describe coping mechanisms you developed that you believe are tied to being an only child.

_____

_____

_____

_____

_____

Thinking Exercise #11

Family dynamics are often revealed fully by how people talk to each other, and how language is used and abused in the household. Using cool processing, recall how each person spoke to the other, and to you.

If this is too anxiety provoking, you're being triggered. STOP!

Journaling Exercise #12

This is a two-part exercise aimed at improving your ability to identify what you're feeling in times of stress.

Part One: Write a description, using as much detail as possible, of a situation that was stressful for you. Here's an example to use as a guide, but feel free to write about any interaction or event that caused you stress or made you feel marginalized or put down:

I introduced my new coworker, Lynne, who's new to the city, to two of my closest friends. We went out together and everyone seemed to get along. Last week, I overheard Lynne telling a colleague that she and my friends went out without me. I told Lynne I was upset and she answered by saying she wasn't either my social secretary or my babysitter and she was under no obligation to invite me.

_____

_____

_____

_____

_____

_____

_____

_____

_____

Part Two: Do this at least a few hours after you've written your description or wait even longer. Then reread what you've written and identify all the emotions evoked by this experience in as much detail and specificity as possible. Here's an example drawn from the one above:

Feelings: First, the sting of betrayal by Lynne. Then feeling betrayed by my friends, along with being angry with them and disappointed by them. Worried about whether I should confront them. Distressed at how my nice gesture became this situation that makes me feel as if I can't do anything right. All of my trust issues bubble up to the surface. I feel used and abandoned.

_____

_____

_____

_____

_____

_____

_____

_____

_____

_____

_____

_____

◈   ◈   ◈

Catchphrase/Journaling Exercise #6

This is another emotional intelligence exercise.

Part One: Study the list of words below and choose those that describe the emotions you're most likely to experience when you're arguing with someone, feeling under fire, or are in some other stressful situation. Circle at least six. This exercise also sheds light on your most consistent style of attachment.

anxious	*scared*	*upset*	*regretful*	*disappointed*
discouraged	*defensive*	*hurt*	*defeated*	*choked*
squashed	*concerned*	*calm*	*indignant*	*comfortable*
annoyed	*angry*	*enraged*	*frustrated*	*disgruntled*
shut-down	*indifferent*	*cold*	*armored*	*guarded*
shamed	*vulnerable*	*unmoved*	*vigilant*	*aloof*
empowered	*superior*	*irritated*	*timid*	*cautious*
committed	*confident*	*secure*	*worried*	*triggered*
hostile	*in control*		*out of control*	*aggressive*

Part Two: Write down the emotions you have chosen on the pages following and then describe the kind of situation that would be most likely to elicit that emotion, such as an argument, a put-down, a rejection, etc. It's normal to have complex emotional responses so feel free to put the words into groups if the emotions are often linked for you.

_____

_____

_____

_____

❖   ❖   ❖

Journaling Exercise #13

Using cool processing as you did in Thinking Exercise #11 on page 51, describe how your mother and father would typically talk to you, being as specific as possible and recalling words and phrases verbatim. Then describe how hearing these words affected you.

IF YOU ARE BEING TRIGGERED, STOP.

❖   ❖   ❖

Mother: _____

_____

_____

_____

_____

_____

_____

Effect: _____

_____

_____

_____

Father: _____

_____

_____

_____

_____

_____

Effect: _____

_____

_____

_____

_____

◈   ◈   ◈

Do you find yourself saying these things to yourself when you're anxious or stressed?
Please list what the voice in your head says and then describe the kind of situation that might elicit this internalized response.

_____

_____

_____

_____

_____

_____

_____

Journaling Exercise #14

This one takes a bit of finesse and you need to judge your own readiness. The goal here is to start identifying the triggers that cause your reactivity and to see whether they are connected to what's happening in the present or whether their source is your childhood past. This exercise comes in two parts; the second part is on pages 58-59 and should be done days after this one.

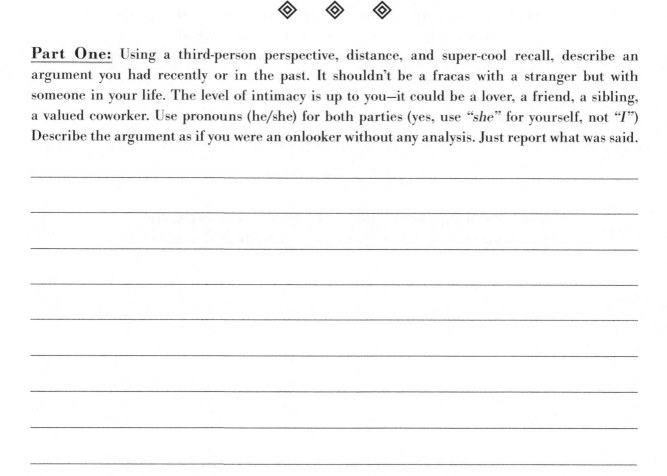

Part One: Using a third-person perspective, distance, and super-cool recall, describe an argument you had recently or in the past. It shouldn't be a fracas with a stranger but with someone in your life. The level of intimacy is up to you—it could be a lover, a friend, a sibling, a valued coworker. Use pronouns (he/she) for both parties (yes, use *"she"* for yourself, not *"I"*) Describe the argument as if you were an onlooker without any analysis. Just report what was said.

_____

_____

_____

_____

_____

_____

_____

_____

Visualization/Catchphrase Exercise #1

Because of the difficulty they have managing emotions and the maladaptive ways of dealing with them—either being flooded with feeling or numbing themselves so they feel little or nothing—many unloved daughters also end up separated from their bodily expressions of emotion. This exercise is designed to help you get in touch with your physical cues—the flush or heat of anger, the tightening of the throat when you're afraid, the way your stomach lurches when you're anxious—to help you better identify what you're feeling.

Visualize a calming, peaceful place—it could be anywhere that makes you feel safe
and grounded—or a person in whose company you feel truly at home.
Or, if you wish, imagine yourself doing something that really gets you in flow;
it could be knitting, swimming, gardening, or anything else
that really makes you feel calm and soothed.
Feel free to use a photograph or an image as an aid to make the visualization
as textured and rich as possible.
Spend as much time concentrating on the visualization—
making it concrete, detail by detail, in your mind—
as you need to until you begin to feel the changes in your body.

Using the spaces below, jot down the words or catchphrases
that capture how it feels to be in your body at this moment.

_____

_____

_____

_____

_____

_____

_____

Part Two: Reread what you wrote on page 57. Think about how you behaved, and ask and answer the following questions of yourself, again from a third-party perspective or as if you were commenting on something that happened to someone else.

Was her behavior reasonable or did she overreact? _____

_____

_____

_____

_____

Was the other person's behavior reasonable or did he/she overstep bounds? _____

_____

_____

_____

_____

Did either party try to manipulate the other through words and gestures? _____

_____

_____

_____

_____

Were there moments when she seemed especially triggered by the other person's words or

gestures? If so, please describe. _____

_____

_____

_____

_____

How might this argument have been changed or resolved differently? _____

_____

_____

_____

_____

_____

◈   ◈   ◈

Journaling Exercise #15

Go back to Catchphrase Exercise #4 on page 26. This exercise is meant to help you begin to connect the dots between your mother's behaviors and the ones you developed in childhood in reaction to her treatment of you. These could be coping strategies or acts of rebellion or submission; the point isn't to judge them as good, bad, or indifferent but to see the connection.

Choose six of the catchphrases you used, copy them below, and then describe the behaviors you developed as a result in full sentences or short phrases. Be kind to yourself, not judgmental.

_____

_____

_____

_____

_____

_____

_____

_____

_____

_____

DISTINGUISH

The moment at which we begin to truly see how the experiences of the past impact and shape our behaviors in the present is often difficult and distressing. Our discoveries are at odds with what we want to believe—that the past is behind us and that we are free of our mothers' influence—but the truth is that we cannot break free until we fully grasp the behaviors we developed in childhood and make them conscious.

What we learned in childhood about how relationships work—and how people behave in intimate settings—shapes us without our awareness. Some of us will have normalized what went on at home; others will know it wasn't "normal" but don't yet have a sense of how it affected them. Most of us will get our first inklings of the lasting effects when we see patterns from childhood echo in adult relationships, find ourselves being treated in ways that are painfully familiar, or experience a series of failed, unhappy-making connections. Most of the time, it won't be obvious how, precisely, the present connects to the past. Some of us will self-sabotage without meaning to and without knowing why, stumbling through life, in the areas of education, work, and relationship. We may have trouble making friends or keeping connections going, or find it hard or impossible to set goals and achieve them. Others will become high achievers but remain plagued by low self-esteem and high self-doubt. Over and over, we may find ourselves drawn to lovers who won't or can't meet our needs.

We must distinguish not just the kinds of people and relationships we're drawn to but the behaviors we adopted in childhood to be able to cope, muddle through, or stay afloat. Then, we will look at how they are still part of our adult lives and how they stop us from growing and changing. By distinguishing those elements, we take the first steps at connecting the dots and seeing the bigger picture.

FOCUS ON PATTERNS

Thinking Exercise #12
Think about three emotionally important relationships you've had as an adult; they could be in the present or in the past. They can be friendships, romantic attachments, familial connections, or mentorships. (The exercise is more revelatory if they are different connections.) In what ways were the relationships similar or different? Look for patterns. Think about the level of intimacy achieved (and whether it was satisfying or problematic), the way conflicts were resolved between you and the other person, and whether the connection was ultimately sustainable.

FOCUS ON FRIENDSHIP

Thinking/Catchphrase/Journaling Exercise #13
Friendships are key to psychological well-being but many unloved daughters have trouble making friends and sustaining connections. The reasons are complex and various, having to do with issues of trust, fear of being hurt or rejected, or problems with intimacy and confiding, especially about your childhood and mother.

How do you feel when you try to make friends? Or when you're in a friendship that's close? Spend some time thinking and then jotting down catchphrases in the spaces below. We've given you some to start with but please add your own as you think.

anxious	*guarded*	*wary*
defensive	*eager to please*	*at ease*
accommodating	*jealous*	*uncomfortable*
empathic	*wanting to belong*	*flexible*
excited	*worried about being used*	*included*
trusting	*scared of rejection*	*open*

_____ _____ _____

_____ _____ _____

_____ _____ _____

What kind of friend did you need or long for as a child? _____

_____

_____

_____

Journaling Exercise #16

Answer the following questions as honestly as you can.

What would you like to change about the friendships you have? _____

_____

_____

_____

_____

What do you contribute to the difficulties you have sustaining friendship? _____

_____

_____

_____

_____

What friendship goals do you need to set for yourself going forward? _____

_____

_____

_____

_____

◈　　◈　　◈

DISTINGUISHING PATTERNS

Thinking/Catchphrase Exercise #14

Think about the kinds of people you tend to surround yourself with, both in friendships and romantic relationships. Are there traits or qualities in men and women alike you are attracted to or do your choices vary by the kind of connection? Think about specific personality traits, characteristic ways of communicating and relating, and what appeals to you. You can circle the catchphrases provided or enter your own in the spaces below.

outgoing	*physically attractive*	*thoughtful*
introspective	*take-charge*	*strong*
kind	*empathic*	*accomplished*
outdoorsy	*athletic*	*intellectual*
uncomplicated	*laid-back*	*charming*
confident	*materially successful*	*articulate*
popular	*quirky*	*opinionated*
quiet/shy	*creative*	*calm*
uncritical	*musical*	*self-involved*
selfish	*hard to get*	*aloof*
challenging	*artistic*	*sweet*

_____ _____ _____

_____ _____ _____

_____ _____ _____

_____ _____ _____

◈   ◈   ◈

FOCUS ON YOU

Journaling Exercise #17

As you begin to distinguish patterns in the relationships you forge, think about what being with these people brings out in you. Describe your interactions with three separate people in the spaces that follow, as accurately and objectively as you can, adapting the point of view of a third party; use the pronoun *"she"* to refer to yourself. Choose one interaction that exemplifies the relationship at its best and one at its worst for each person. Ask yourself whether this is your best self, your worst self, or something in between.

Relationship with _____

Best Interaction: _____

_____

_____

_____

_____

Worst Interaction: _____

_____

_____

_____

_____

Relationship with _____

Best Interaction: _____

_____

_____

_____

_____

Worst Interaction: _____

_____

_____

_____

_____

Relationship with _____

Best Interaction: _____

_____

_____

_____

_____

Worst Interaction: _____

_____

_____

_____

_____

◈   ◈   ◈

WORKING MODELS IN THE PRESENT

Journaling Exercise #18

It's one thing to understand your attachment style in the abstract (see page 16); it's another to recognize the predominant style in action. Using these questions as prompts, do some thinking before you write and then answer as fully as you can, in complete sentences.

Is there an underlying pattern to the relationships I choose to be in? _____

_____

_____

_____

_____

Are my reactions and emotional responses basically the same in every relationship, no matter how different the person I'm with is?

_____

_____

_____

_____

_____

*Am I attracted to the same kind of person again and again? Explain.*_____

_____

_____

_____

_____

Are there basic problems I have in every relationship? What are they? _____

_____

_____

_____

_____

_____

_____

_____

ATTACHMENT STYLES OF CLOSE OTHERS

Journaling Exercise #19

No, this isn't an invitation to play amateur psychologist but one to really focus on how the people you choose to be with behave in broad-stroke ways. It's divided into two parts: one for a close friend and the other for a romantic partner. Rely on your knowledge and experience of the person as well as what you know about her or his childhood experiences, whether she or he is comfortable with her or himself and confident without needing to bulldoze you and others, and the like. Spend time thinking before writing in full sentences.

Part One: Close Friend's Attachment Style

Is this a relationship of equals? If so, why? If not, why? _____

_____

_____

_____

_____

_____

_____

How do the two of you make plans? Is one person in control? _____

_____

_____

_____

_____

_____

_____

Is he/she she a good listener? An empath?

_____

_____

_____

_____

_____

Does he/she have reasonable confidence and self-esteem? _____

_____

_____

_____

_____

_____

_____

How do his/her personality and behavior affect your relationship? _____

_____

_____

_____

_____

_____

_____

How does he/she handle conflict?

_____

_____

_____

_____

_____

_____

How do you and he/she handle disagreements? _____

_____

_____

_____

_____

_____

Do you feel you can trust him/her implicitly? Please explain. _____

_____

_____

_____

_____

_____

How close do you think you are and why?

_____

_____

_____

_____

_____

_____

Now that you've begun to see your own patterns of behavior, are there things you understand

that you didn't before? Explain in detail. _____

_____

_____

_____

_____

_____

_____

_____

_____

_____

◈   ◈   ◈

Part Two: Romantic Partner Attachment Style

What behaviors or traits most define him? Please describe. _____

_____

_____

_____

_____

_____

_____

Are these the very same things that attracted you to him? Please explain. _____

_____

_____

_____

_____

_____

_____

_____

How does your relational style mesh with his? Please describe and explain. _____

_____

_____

_____

_____

_____

_____

Describe how the two of you make decisions. Were they joint or was there a leader and a follower? Please describe. _____

_____

_____

_____

_____

_____

Why are you close? What are the bonds that keep you close? _____

_____

_____

_____

_____

_____

_____

_____

_____

_____

_____

_____

_____

By examining these patterns, are there things you understand that you didn't before?

_____

_____

_____

_____

_____

_____

_____

_____

_____

◈   ◈   ◈

YOU AND INTIMACY

Thinking/Journaling Exercise #20

Since the culture romanticizes being consumed by a relationship—which isn't healthy, by the way—many of us have trouble acknowledging our problems with intimacy, or even understanding the degree to which other people are capable of intimacy. Yet, knowing yourself requires that you know and explore your own limits so you can decide whether they need revision or expansion. Think first and then answer below.

What role does sexual intimacy play in your relationships? How important or unimportant

is it? _____

_____

_____

_____

_____

Do you and your partner(s) argue about sex? If so, why?

_____

_____

_____

_____

_____

_____

Do you get anxious when your partner doesn't want to make love? Why? _____

_____

_____

_____

_____

_____

_____

Is sex reassurance that you're loved or something else? _____

_____

_____

_____

_____

_____

Do your lovers complain that you're too distant? Or too clingy?

_____

_____

_____

_____

_____

◈　　◈　　◈

FOCUS: YOUR ROLE IN CONFLICT

Journaling Exercise #21

Marital expert John Gottman has observed that it's not whether partners fight that matters but *how* they argue that does. Daughters of unloving mothers are often fearful of conflict, choosing to silence themselves or to please and appease to avoid the issue. Others are highly reactive and even combative especially when they feel threatened. Understanding how you behave when there's disagreement—minor or major in nature—is an important part of self-knowledge.

How did you react to conflict as a child? _____

_____

_____

_____

_____

How did you react to conflict as a teenager? _____

_____

_____

_____

_____

_____

As an adult, are you able to discuss differences in opinion calmly? Please explain.

_____

_____

_____

_____

_____

Do you or your partner routinely engage in stonewalling, personalized criticism, or gaslighting? Answer in detail. _____

_____

_____

_____

_____

_____

Are these familiar patterns, known from childhood? Please elaborate. _____

_____

_____

_____

_____

_____

How has your style of managing conflict shaped your intimate relationships?

_____

_____

_____

_____

_____

_____

_____

What do you think you need to learn about conflict resolution? Be as specific as possible.

_____

_____

_____

_____

_____

_____

_____

_____

◈   ◈   ◈

YOU AND STRESS

Thinking/Catchphrase Exercise #15
Do different kinds of stress evoke different responses in you? Distinguishing the specific situations that produce specific and familiar emotional responses and behaviors is an important step in healing.

Write your own catchphrases and words beneath each of the highlighted moments of stress, or use the ones listed below.

frantic	*calm*	*thoughtful*
withdrawn	*flooded*	*angry*
tongue-tied	*defensive*	*removed*
emotionless	*cold*	*devastated*
hysterical	*armored*	*rational*
in charge	*afraid*	*undone*
tearful	*passive*	*despairing*
victimized	*withdrawn*	*ready to flee*
charged-up	*hurt*	*frozen*
energized	*unable to act*	*aggressive*

Feeling excluded, abandoned, or rejected

_____

_____

_____

_____

Arguing/fighting

_____

_____

_____

_____

Being personally criticized

_____

_____

_____

_____

Being put down or marginalized

_____   _____

_____   _____

_____   _____

_____   _____

Feeling frustrated or misunderstood

_____   _____

_____   _____

_____   _____

_____   _____

Being shut out or stonewalled

_____   _____

_____   _____

_____   _____

_____   _____

Facing a challenge

_____   _____

_____   _____

_____   _____

_____   _____

Making a pivotal decision

_____   _____

_____   _____

_____   _____

_____   _____

Confronting a possible failure

_____   _____

_____   _____

_____   _____

_____   _____

◈   ◈   ◈

Visualization Exercise #2

Choose a time when you can do this undisturbed and do it in a place that calms you.
Turn your phone off.

❋   ❋   ❋

Visualize what you would consider an ideal friendship or romantic connection.
How would the person act?
What would the two of you be doing together?
How would you act with this person?
What changes in yourself would you see if you were in his or her company?

❋   ❋   ❋

If you're unable to visualize or imagine such a relationship, that, too, is revelatory.

◈   ◈   ◈

DISARM

When we begin to bring our unconscious patterns of behavior into conscious awareness marks a turning point in our development. Once we see our actions and reactions as rooted in our childhood experiences, we begin to fathom how they function in the day-to-day. It's at that moment that we can begin to dismantle and disarm them and embark on changing ourselves. Once they are no longer automatic—triggers ready to be pulled—new ways of acting become possible.

Disarming requires that we understand how the brain works, both generally and ours specifically. The brain takes shortcuts and we need to be familiar with all of them as we examine our behaviors and specifically what drives them. To dig deeper, we need to understand cues in the environment and how we react.

The process of disarming can be both disconcerting and frustrating at times. We may find to our dismay that our old habits of mind and ways of seeing are the biggest obstacles to our peace and happiness, and it takes special effort not to blame ourselves. Old wounds may reopen, especially as we begin to better understand our own role in our current relationships, including those with our mothers. Facing what I call the dance of denial and understanding how it has functioned in our lives is of key importance. We have to take responsibility for what we bring and have brought to the party without falling into the trap of self-blaming and criticism.

Only by disarming our automatic responses can we begin to behave differently and find new emotional opportunities for ourselves. This part of the path is arduous but necessary and can be frustrating. These old ways of coping have to be identified and pulled out by the roots before we can plant new behaviors to live happier and more fulfilled lives. The push is clear: to make the unconscious conscious.

THE DANCE OF DENIAL

Thinking/Catchphrase Exercise #16

Many of us remain mired in the core conflict, either still trying to get our mothers' love or somehow keep the peace; often, that includes denying, rationalizing, excusing, or normalizing the things our mothers do and say. It's what I call *the dance of denial*. As you think about your own behaviors, consider the following questions and, after you've spent time thinking, write them down. Your answers can serve as helpful reminders in the future.

Your motivation: Fear of losing family ties? Shame in giving up hope? Societal criticism? Continued hopefulness that the relationship could be salvaged? Fear of ending up alone? Or was it something else?

_____

_____

_____

_____

_____

_____

Continuing effect on you: Has your continued struggle with the relationship had ripple effects? Is thinking that the relationship can be fixed realistic? Be honest.

_____

_____

_____

_____

_____

_____

Effect on your behaviors: Do you find yourself falling into old patterns—of feeling frantic to please or extremely anxious? Describe how this affects you in the day-to-day and in your adult relationships.

_____

_____

_____

_____

_____

Understanding triggers: Do you still find yourself making excuses for your mother or telling yourself that your feelings aren't legitimate? Do you know the source for this reaction or can you guess?

_____

_____

_____

_____

_____

Strategizing: What do you think you need to do to stop participating in the dance of denial? Be as specific as you can be about the steps you'll take.

_____

_____

_____

_____

_____

COPING WITH THE CORE CONFLICT

Journaling Exercise #22

This conflict runs deep and is rarely resolved by a single epiphany; it has to be tackled over time and usually is. Even so, it may be ongoing even after you've decided on a course of action. The battle is progressive because it involves becoming more convinced of your own worth and need to protect yourself, on the one hand, and, on the other, your growing realism about your mother's capacity to love you. Think first and then answer the prompts.

Which part of the core conflict do you struggle with most? _____

_____

_____

_____

_____

What held or still holds you in place? Describe your inner thoughts. _____

_____

_____

_____

_____

What, if anything, frightens you about the choices ahead? _____

_____

_____

_____

_____

Does recognizing the conflict make you feel powerless or empowered?

_____

_____

_____

_____

_____

Do you continually second-guess your actions and reactions? _____

_____

_____

_____

_____

_____

Use the lines below to explore your thoughts and feelings, whether you are still struggling with the relationship or if you've gone low- or no-contact. Be as specific as possible.

_____

_____

_____

_____

_____

_____

_____

◈　　◈　　◈

GETTING A BEAD ON YOUR REACTIVITY

Doing a thorough inventory of how you respond to cues in the environment—things said and things left unsaid, gestures and actions—as well as your own sensitivity to those cues is central to knowing yourself and understanding which behaviors no longer stand you in good stead. All of the following exercises are meant to help you push forward with self-examination that is unflinching but also not filled with self-blame.

Thinking/Journaling Exercise #23

Pick a recent situation that evoked a strong emotional reaction. It could be a fight or argument, a moment at which you felt excluded or mocked, something that made you jealous or frightened, or any other interaction that made you emotionally reactive. Write using a detached third-person perspective but use the pronoun *"I."*

Describe the situation as completely as you can. _____

_____

_____

_____

_____

_____

_____

What triggered your response? _____

_____

_____

_____

_____

_____

Describe your emotions as completely and precisely as you can with complexity in mind, and say why you felt as you did. _____

_____

_____

_____

_____

_____

In retrospect, were there other ways you might have responded? Please discuss.

_____

_____

_____

_____

_____

How much of your reactivity had to do with past experiences? Discuss in detail.

_____

_____

_____

_____

_____

◈　　◈　　◈

THE POWER OF PRIMES, CUES, AND TRIGGERS

Thinking/Catchphrase Exercise #17

Knowing which primes, cues, and triggers are likely to affect your mood and reactions is an important piece of self-knowledge. Please think about each of these and then fill in what comes to mind in the spaces below.

Situational cues: Do large gatherings or parties make you reactive? Are you sensitive to ambiance and décor, lighting and color, or noise levels? Think about what stresses you and what soothes you and write down what comes to mind. Be as detailed as possible.

Stress

_____

_____

_____

_____

Soothe

_____

_____

_____

_____

Interpersonal cues: When you meet someone for the first time, what do you focus on and what do you pay attention to? Do you judge people by their appearance, their self-presentation, or something else? When you interact with someone, are you more focused on their words, their facial expressions, their body language, or tone of voice? What is likely to produce a positive or negative response in you?

Stress

_____

_____

_____

_____

Soothe

_____

_____

_____

_____

Are there specific behaviors that trigger emotional responses in you (for example, someone rolling her/his eyes at you, frowning or scowling, or raising his/her voice or yelling)? List the behaviors and then, as completely as you can, describe your response.

Behavior _____

_____

_____

_____

Behavior _____

_____

_____

_____

Behavior _____

_____

_____

_____

Behavior _____

_____

_____

_____

LISTENING TO YOUR BODY

Many unloved daughters don't just push off from their emotions or have difficulty managing them; in addition, they often feel out of sync with or disconnected from their bodies. Rather than use the physical sensations that accompany strong or even uncomfortable feelings as a tool of emotional intelligence—"*I am feeling my chest tighten because I'm anxious,*" "*I can't breathe because I'm scared*"—they may simply ignore them. In a similar way, they may also not be able to see that some physical symptoms—a sudden headache, a feeling of being somehow "*off*" in their bodies, back pain—may be the result of strong emotions they're experiencing or could be the result of an unconscious emotional response to something in the present that evokes a childhood experience.

Journaling Exercise #24
This exercise has four separate parts, one of which requires you to deliberately feel stressed, and others which ask you to "*hot process*" and recall physical feelings.

STOP IMMEDIATELY IF YOU FEEL OVERWHELMED.

Part One: Recall an incident from your childhood that typified your relationship to your mother; it could be one you've journaled about or one you haven't. Use the lines below to explore how your childhood self responded physically to feeling hurt or marginalized. Did you go to bed and curl up or did you read or distract yourself? Can you remember the physical responses you had at the time? Please describe and comment on whether this was typical of you as a girl.

_____

_____

_____

_____

_____

Part Two: Were you mocked for crying, tearing up, or showing your emotions as a child? If so, write about what you did to deal with your physical responses and how this behavior made you feel.

_____

_____

_____

_____

_____

_____

Part Three: Were you subject to body shaming? Called fat, derided for how parts of your body looked, or called ugly? Are there parts of your body that evoke negative emotion? Please explore using cool processing in the space below.

_____

_____

_____

_____

_____

Part Four: Begin with a calming visualization, as described on page 58; you may want to reread your description of what your body felt like when you were calm. Now, visualize a stressful situation or demanding person, paying close attention to the changes in your body. Calm yourself again by using breathing or visualization and then describe your physical feelings and thoughts as you visualized the stressful situation.

_____

_____

_____

_____

_____

REJECTION SENSITIVITY

Thinking/Journaling Exercise #25

Following are various scenarios that could trigger someone who has rejection sensitivity. You need to know how reactive and prone to reading in you are. Think about each and write down in the space below how you would act, what you would feel, and the explanation you would come up with. Feel free to add in personal scenarios at the end.

You leave someone a message and she or he doesn't call back.

_____

_____

_____

_____

_____

You learn you were the last person invited to a party.

_____

_____

_____

_____

Your coworker or neighbor seems distant or preoccupied during your chat or visit.

_____

_____

_____

_____

Your girlfriend constantly ignores the advice you give her.

_____

_____

_____

_____

You're giving a party and wondering why some people aren't coming.

_____

_____

_____

_____

Two of your friends are going to lunch together and didn't invite you.

_____

_____

_____

_____

Your close other is on a business trip and doesn't call you all day.

_____

_____

_____

_____

You show someone something you're proud of and he or she says very little.

_____

_____

_____

_____

You give a friend a gift and she barely acknowledges it.

_____

_____

_____

_____

People are laughing at a joke and you think it may be about you.

_____

_____

_____

_____

You see an acquaintance at the store but she doesn't acknowledge you.

_____

_____

_____

_____

Your spouse/boyfriend is in a bad mood and doesn't say much.

_____

_____

_____

_____

You post a photo or comment on social media and no one responds or likes it.

_____

_____

_____

_____

Your own scenarios:

_____

_____

_____

_____

_____

_____

_____

_____

_____

❖   ❖   ❖

HABITS OF MIND (EVERYONE'S, BUT ESPECIALLY YOURS)

The tendency of women to ruminate more than men, the power of intermittent reinforcement, and the limits of focus (inattentional blindness) are well known in scientific research. The following exercises are meant to clarify which of these habits of mind plays a role in keeping you stuck.

Thinking/Journaling Exercise #26

Do you end up awake in the middle of the night or do you tend to obsess over details when you're stressed? Discovering why you ruminate and what kinds of situations trigger this behavior can help you come up with techniques to stop it. The first prompt is a question; the ones that follow are reflections.

Do you ruminate more about things that have happened or things that may happen, or both? Please think and then answer in depth.

_____

_____

_____

_____

_____

_____

I'm most likely to ruminate when _____

_____

_____

_____

_____

_____

Ruminative loops make me feel _____

_____

_____

_____

_____

_____

Describe the last such ruminative loop you were in and its causes _____

_____

_____

_____

_____

_____

Why do you think you can't stop ruminating? _____

_____

_____

_____

_____

◈   ◈   ◈

INTERMITTENT REINFORCEMENT

Thinking/Journaling Exercise #27

Think about how getting what you want some of the time but not all the time (yes, intermittent reinforcement) has played a role in your decision-making and whether you stay in or leave a relationship or situation. Examples of intermittent reinforcement include rare occasions when you feel heard (even though you're usually ignored), the absence of hurtful behavior, which you interpret as a positive sign, or any event or behavior you respond to as a signal of a real change of heart in another. It is dangerously powerful as well as emotionally confusing.

In relationships, I become overly optimistic when _____

_____

_____

_____

I have changed my mind about leaving or staying when _____

_____

_____

_____

_____

My indecision has been fed by moments like these: _____

_____

_____

_____

I tend to overemphasize the importance of these kinds of interactions because _____

_____

_____

_____

I think this kind of reinforcement has kept me _____

_____

_____

_____

If you are anxiously attached or rejection sensitive, how has this kind of reinforcement

affected your behavior? _____

_____

_____

_____

_____

◈   ◈   ◈

STUCK ON DETAILS

Thinking/Journaling Exercise #28

In addition to replaying events and encounters in your head (rumination), do you also tend to focus on details, even obsessively? That can stop you from seeing the bigger picture and cloud your thinking; this habit of mind is called *inattentional blindness*.

How prone are you to read into what someone says? Do you take statements at face value or do you analyze every word? Please give an example of when this habit tripped you up.

_____

_____

_____

_____

_____

When you think about an event or an encounter, do you tend to focus on the positive, the negative, or a balance of both? Please describe two situations in detail, writing about how your thinking proceeded.

*Situation #1*_____

_____

_____

_____

_____

*Situation #2*_____

_____

_____

_____

_____

When you think about an event or encounter that didn't end well, are you able to look at it objectively or do you focus on the details that are most personal?

_____

_____

_____

_____

_____

◈   ◈   ◈

USING STOP, LOOK, LISTEN

Thinking Exercise #18

Examining how our unconscious patterns come into play is vital to our self-understanding; learning how to disarm those automatic reactions is crucial to moving forward. One way is to take a mental time-out when you are under stress and to *stop* reacting, to *look* at the situation you're in as if it's happening to someone else, and to *listen* to what's being said and to your conscious thoughts as an objective onlooker. You may have to remove yourself physically from the situation the first few times you do this.

Think about a recent disagreement or heated argument you had or some other stressful situation when you couldn't calm down and reacted in the moment by either withdrawing, flooding, or lashing out defensively. Imagine if you'd availed yourself of the *Stop, Look, Listen* technique and then answer the following.

Looking back, what do you see about your behavior and reactivity that you couldn't in the

moment? _____

_____

_____

_____

_____

How would using Stop, Look, Listen have changed both the dynamic and the outcome?

_____

_____

_____

_____

_____

_____

Can you name the emotional triggers and connect them to your behaviors? Explain in

detail. _____

_____

_____

_____

_____

What new information have you gleaned about your reactivity? _____

_____

_____

_____

_____

_____

Has your perspective on this disagreement changed? Describe and explain. _____

_____

_____

_____

_____

_____

Thinking/Journaling Exercise #29

Imagine and then write about two separate situations that you think would trigger your reactivity; they can be drawn from experience or made up or a combination of both. Then describe how you would use **Stop, Look, Listen** to manage your emotions and discuss the possible outcome.

Situation #1

_____

_____

_____

_____

_____

_____

_____

_____

_____

Situation #2

_____

_____

_____

_____

_____

_____

_____

_____

_____

◈　　◈　　◈

EMOTIONAL INVENTORY

Thinking/Journaling Exercise #30

Spend some time thinking about how you manage emotions—are you primarily avoidant or anxious?—and think about how changing your emotional skill set would change your life. Answer the following questions and then write a description of what you think you need to learn for future growth.

How skilled am I at identifying and labeling emotions? _____

_____

_____

_____

_____

What aspect of identifying what I'm feeling is hardest for me? _____

_____

_____

_____

_____

How good am I at identifying what I'm feeling in the present? _____

_____

_____

_____

_____

Does hindsight help me untangle my feelings?

_____

_____

_____

_____

_____

_____

How good am I at anticipating how I will feel in the future? _____

_____

_____

_____

_____

_____

_____

How do my moods influence my ability to know what I'm feeling? _____

_____

_____

_____

_____

_____

_____

RECLAIM

Once we've begun to understand how to disarm the maladaptive strategies we adopted to get through childhood, it's time to move toward reclaiming our authentic selves, free of influence. This is the self who will learn to shun toxic and manipulative behaviors. This is the self who will be at ease with her own distinctive voice. This is the self who sets her own sights for the future. This is the self *empowered*. But this road out isn't easy. Many of us will find that the process is bumpy rather than smooth, characterized by fits and starts, at a frustrating pace of two steps forward and one step back.

It's to be expected that it's hard to unlearn what you learned during the time your brain was at its most receptive and you were a needy child. You will have to summon up reserves of patience and a refusal to become frustrated when both are hard to come by. The two most difficult tasks at hand are the unlearning of the habit of self-criticism and learning to be compassionate toward yourself. These are hard for all unloved daughters and they require exertion and effort,

Still, this is the moment at which the light beckons. When we do the work for new opportunities in how we think, react, and feel, it's all potentially glorious.

There's loss and letting go involved in the process because that's exactly what unlearning entails. Your behaviors and choices may make you miserable but they are comfortable and familiar. This is new territory, which may stretch you in ways that feel initially uncomfortable, as you challenge old ways of thinking, take on new ones, start setting goals, and take on the risk of failure. The earth may shake under your feet from time to time but you have to understand you're finally moving in the direction of consistently stable ground. Really.

There's a hill to be climbed and you must believe that you are ready to climb it. If you falter, go back to earlier exercises in the book and do them again. You'll get there. Trust me on that. Better still, trust *you* on that.

ENDING PLEASING AND APPEASING

Thinking Exercise #19

Using the if/then approach, think about the strategies you'll adopt when you next deal with manipulative or toxic people in your life. Pay specific attention to the degree to which you find yourself taking the appease/please role in conflict or how you tend to normalize these kinds of behaviors. Be as specific as you can be in preparation for the next journaling exercise.

◈　◈　◈

DEALING WITH TOXIC BEHAVIOR

Journaling Exercise #31

Describe in detail a run-in you had with someone who was stonewalling, being verbally abusive, or behaving in some other toxic or controlling manner. After you've described the incident, answer the questions below as honestly as you can.

_____

_____

_____

_____

_____

Do you see familiar old patterns in your behavior? Name them. _____

_____

_____

_____

_____

Were you able to adopt new strategies? Please explain.

_____

_____

_____

_____

_____

_____

If you were a bystander, how would you advise you to better handle it? _____

_____

_____

_____

_____

_____

◈　　◈　　◈

NAMING FEELINGS

Thinking/Catchphrase Exercise #20

Honing your skills to know what you are feeling in the moment not only permits you to manage your emotions but also allows you to see your behavior in another context; strengthening your emotional intelligence remains an important objective. Describe four emotionally laden incidents and then, in the spaces on the next pages, name your emotions and describe why you felt as you did. Here's an example:

Situation: We were arguing about money and I started to cry and he said, "Why are you incapable of being an adult? Your sensitivity makes it impossible to discuss anything." Then he left the room and I melted down.

What I Felt: Anxiety, shame, fear, abandoned, angry, frustrated, upset

Why I Felt That Way: I feel blamed and defensive when we talk about money. He's so much more careful than I am. But he gets upset when I cry and he's not wrong. We should be able to talk without my overreacting to criticism.

Situation #1: _____

_____

_____

What I felt: _____

_____

Why I felt that way: _____

_____

_____

Situation #2: _____

_____

_____

What I felt: _____

_____

Why I felt that way: _____

_____

_____

Situation #3: _____

_____

_____

What I felt: _____

_____

Why I felt that way: _____

_____

_____

Situation #4: _____

_____

_____

What I felt: _____

_____

Why I felt that way: _____

_____

_____

◈   ◈   ◈

USING COGNITIVE REAPPRAISAL

Thinking/Journaling Exercise #32
Describe a situation in which you felt emotionally threatened and focus on why you felt as you did, with attention to emotional triggers.

_____

_____

_____

_____

_____

_____

Now imagine how you might have behaved and the ways in which the situation would have been different had you used cognitive reappraisal. Describe the specific strategies you could have taken.

_____

_____

_____

_____

_____

_____

◈   ◈   ◈

SHUTTING DOWN THE CRITICAL TAPE

Thinking/Journaling Exercise #33
When you're challenged, threatened, or stressed, what kind of self-critical statements float to the top? Reflect and then write down the eight most common thoughts that dominate.

That I am

_____

_____

That I always

_____

_____

That I never

_____

_____

That I won't be able to

_____

_____

Now, in the spaces below, challenge and countermand those statements with your own observations about your abilities, traits, and character,

I am able to

_____

_____

I am skilled at

_____

_____

I am capable of

_____

_____

My strengths are

_____

_____

Weaknesses I need to work on

_____

_____

SELF-TALK

Thinking/Journaling Exercise #34

Getting in the habit of using positive reinforcement to defang self-criticism and to boost your self-esteem is a smart thing to do. Think about your best qualities and make them into statements. They need not be Pollyanna-positive but can be realistic. Here's mine: *"I may be a lousy housekeeper but I am a good cook and an even better writer."*

Use your own words or choose from the suggestions below:

kind	*empathic*	*spirited*	*unique*
creative	*original*	*intelligent*	*thoughtful*
diligent	*honest*	*freethinking*	*energetic*
enthusiastic	*funny*	*skilled*	*motivated*
loyal	*flexible*	*dogged*	*quirky*
steady	*patient*	*giving*	*uncritical*
generous	*helpful*	*supportive*	*understanding*
listener	*trustworthy*	*handy*	*chef*
seamstress	*knitter*	*painter*	*flower arranger*
skier	*dancer*	*singer*	*tennis player*
swimmer	*writer*	*hostess*	*worker*
friend	*colleague*	*neighbor*	*gardener*

Use the spaces below and on the next page to come up with ten self-talk statements.

1. _____

_____

2. _____

_____

3. _____

_____

4. _____

_____

5. _____

6. _____

_____

7. _____

_____

8. _____

_____

9. _____

_____

10. _____

_____

EMOTIONAL SELF-EXPLORATION

Thinking/Journaling Exercise #35

Increasing your ability to name your emotions and to identify your moods will put you more in command of your behaviors by reducing your reactivity and putting your higher brain—the thinking part—in charge. To do this exercise, you will need a pocket notebook to carry with you or you can make mental notes and then write down your observations below. The goal here is to learn to pay attention to shifts in your emotions or changes in mood. Record at least six such moments. An example: *"I was excited to see my friend but she ran late, and I sat there alone for more than thirty minutes. I went from being happy to feeling frustrated to angry and when she laughed it off, I felt hurt."* Track the changes in your emotions (in this case, from happy to hurt) and give reasons for the shift.

_____

_____

_____

EXPLORING YOUR BELIEFS ABOUT THE SELF

Research shows that what you believe about character and personality—whether you think they're fixed or malleable, set in stone or fluid—influences both behavior and reactivity in many ways. Getting a bead on what you really believe is important.

Thinking/Journaling Exercise #36
Reflect on whether you believe you can actually change your behavior in meaningful ways if you choose to—and that other people can, too—before you answer the following questions.

How much does conscious choice affect the ability to change? _____

_____

_____

_____

_____

Do you believe you can change yourself? Explain in detail. _____

_____

_____

_____

_____

If you're not sure you can change, state the reasons why, and specify which traits are fixed.

_____

_____

_____

_____

_____

If you think you can change, explain what will be needed.

_____

_____

_____

_____

Do your close intimates believe that personality is fluid? Explain. _____

_____

_____

_____

_____

Are you influenced by what your close intimates think? Answer in detail. _____

_____

_____

_____

_____

Do you think your beliefs consciously or unconsciously inform your decisions and behaviors?

_____

_____

_____

_____

If you believe personality is more fixed than not, explain how that affects you.

_____

_____

_____

_____

_____

If you believe personality is malleable, explain how that affects you. _____

_____

_____

_____

_____

REJECTION SENSITIVITY

Thinking/Journaling Exercise #37

Learning to regulate your sensitivity is one way of eliminating some of the drama in your relationships, especially if you display an anxious/preoccupied style of attachment. Think about a situation that triggered your fear of rejection and then, in the spaces below, come up with strategies you will use in the future to deal with it. This could include refocusing, cognitive reappraisal, etc.

_____

_____

_____

_____

_____

LEARNING SELF-COMPASSION

Is it the culture's negative take on self-love as a bad thing (ending up too narcissistic, focused on yourself) that trips us up when we try to display compassion toward ourselves or is it the endless loop of self-criticism that gets in the way? Keep in mind, as you proceed, that self-compassion isn't self-pity or feeling sad that you were victimized. Self-compassion includes suspending judgment and experiencing your own humanity.

Journaling Exercise #38

Find a photo of yourself, preferably as a child or young girl, and spend time looking at it. Bring to mind things that your mother (and other family members, if that applies) said about that little girl. Now, in the space below, look at that girl and describe her as you remember her, focusing on what she loved to do, how she smiled and felt joy, and anything else that comes to mind about the little girl you were, the one your mother was incapable of seeing.

_____

_____

_____

_____

_____

_____

_____

_____

_____

_____

SELF-TALK AND COMPASSION

Thinking/Journaling Exercise #39

Go back to the ten self-talk statements you wrote on pages 124-125. Record each of those statements in the spaces below and then expand upon them, writing what they say about you and how you are trying to live your life, even if you don't always meet with success. Write as though you are a third party who has empathy for you, your triumphs, and your struggles.

1. _____

_____

_____

_____

2. _____

_____

_____

_____

3. _____

_____

_____

_____

4. _____

_____

_____

_____

5. _____

_____

6. _____

7. _____

8. _____

9. _____

10. _____

SELF-COMPASSION AS A GOAL

Thinking/Journaling Exercise #40

Writing your goals down has been shown to increase clarity, motivation, and implementation, and this exercise will help you both in goal-setting generally and inculcating self-compassion. Tackle the ways in which you fail to be self-compassionate by setting five goals to overcome those specific failures.

Goal: _____

_____

_____

_____

_____

Goal: _____

_____

_____

_____

_____

Goal: _____

_____

_____

_____

_____

Goal: _____

_____

_____

_____

_____

_____

Goal: _____

_____

_____

_____

_____

_____

Visualization Exercise #3

Visualize the child you were and imagine the mother you needed and wanted.
Draw on the qualities you've seen in other women and men
—their ability to listen, to nurture, to be kind—
especially the loving mothers of friends or caring people you've run into.
Create an image you can draw on in times of stress;
use your imagination to fill in the details.

GOAL-SETTING

Thinking/Journaling Exercise #41

Setting your sights on the future is important, as is working on strengthening your motivation to find new paths and ways of living. This is especially true if you've been largely avoidant because of your fear of failure. This exercise is divided into three parts and each part should, in the best of all possible worlds, be done a few days apart.

Part One: Goal-Setting

Focus on four goals you want to achieve in the near future and two you hope to achieve in the next year or so. They can be general or very specific, in the realm of relationships (make new friends, strengthen my relationship to my spouse or partner), specifically about your mother and family of origin (set new boundaries, write Mom a letter), work related (be more direct at work, learn to code or acquire a specific skill), or personal (build my self-confidence, get better at dealing with my anger). Make sure that your goals are congruent and that you have the skill set to achieve them. If you don't, you will need to set interim goals first.

In the spaces below, set your goals, and describe the steps you'll take and the strategies you'll adopt as specifically as you can.

Near-Term Goal: _____

_____

_____

_____

_____

Near-Term Goal: _____

_____

_____

_____

_____

Near-Term Goal: _____

_____

_____

_____

_____

Near-Term Goal: _____

_____

_____

_____

_____

Long-Term Goal: _____

_____

_____

_____

_____

Long-Term Goal: _____

_____

_____

_____

_____

Part Two: Motivating Yourself

Write down three self-talk statements you will use if you experience disappointment or a setback.

_1._ _____

_____

_____

_____

_2._ _____

_____

_____

_____

_3._ _____

_____

_____

_____

Spend time thinking about how you will cheerlead yourself in your goal pursuit and what you'll do proactively to avoid fear of failure and then write about it.

_____

_____

_____

_____

_____

_____

Part Three: Troubleshooting with If/Then Thinking

Fear of failure and the inability to recover from setbacks are often hallmarks of the unloved daughter and great impediments when it comes to goal-setting and achievement. If/then thinking makes you proactive as you anticipate glitches and even setbacks, formulating a Plan B if Plan A doesn't work. This is both mental and emotional preparation, which permits you to pivot rather than flounder when there's a glitch. Go back to the short-term goals and strategies you outlined on pages 135-136 and, using if/then thinking, troubleshoot.

If I fall short of reaching my objectives, I will then _____

_____

_____

_____

_____

_____

_____

Alternative strategies for my first short-term goal are _____

_____

_____

_____

_____

_____

_____

Plan B for my second near-future goal is _____

_____

_____

_____

_____

_____

_____

_____

If my third short-term goal is thwarted, I will then _____

_____

_____

_____

_____

_____

Possible work-arounds for my fourth goal are _____

_____

_____

_____

_____

_____

_____

_____

REDIRECT

It's at this stage of the process that you take the reins in hand and begin to redirect your life, making changes as you see fit to increase your happiness and well-being. This moment tests your newfound trust in yourself and forces you to rely on both your thoughts and perceptions. For many, this part of the journey consists of baby steps and even a pattern of two steps forward, one step back. This is normal and you will have to be patient with yourself and not let the pace discourage you. Eventually, with practice and determination, those little steps become strides. Claiming this agency may feel uncomfortable at first, especially if you've been largely motivated by avoidance, but you will settle in over time.

Chief among the decisions you'll be dealing with is how to manage your relationship to your mother (and the rest of your family of origin). In the pages ahead, you'll be encouraged to do some deep thinking and self-examination so that the road you choose is the right one for you. This is also the time to take a personal inventory of all your relationships and decide which ones are those that help you thrive and be your best possible self and which give you the most pleasure and joy. Along the way, you may find yourself learning new ways to connect with greater intimacy and stronger communication as you begin to let go of self-limiting behaviors and embrace those that expand the self.

Growth and change take effort and diligence and aren't easy. The seed planted has to push through the soil forcefully to become a flower, and this process isn't any different. Staying aware of healthy boundaries—having your own respected and respecting those of others—is a task to be taken on, as is redefining the self, going from the unloved daughter to a woman with a voice.

But along with effort, there is also exhilaration, a lifting of a long-carried but unseen weight, and the beckoning of the light in the distance.

LIFE AHEAD

Journaling Exercise #42

Spend some time thinking about the behaviors and aspects of your life you'd like to change. Now narrow them down to two short-term goals and two long-term goals for each. For example, changes to behavior could include *"Handling anxiety better," "Procrastinating less," "Being more assertive," "Being a better listener instead of reactive."* Life changes could include goals in all of the domains of your life such as *"Spending more time with friends," "Finding a more fulfilling job," "Expanding my social circle," "Taking more chances and doing new things," "Becoming more active in my community."*

Write down your goals in detail below along with how you plan to achieve them.

*Short-Term Goal:*_____

Plan: _____

_____

_____

_____

*Short-Term Goal:*_____

Plan: _____

_____

_____

_____

Long-Term Goal: _____

Plan: _____

_____

_____

_____

Long-Term Goal: _____

Plan: _____

_____

_____

_____

◈   ◈   ◈

TAKING CHARGE, NAMING FEELINGS

Thinking/Catchphrase Exercise #21

As you consider how to manage your relationship to your mother (and, inevitably, the rest of your family of origin), what thoughts float into your head? What do you feel in the moment? Study the list below and circle those that fit; feel free to add in more in the slots provided. Keep in mind that feeling ambivalent at some level goes with the territory so don't be surprised if some choices contradict others.

anxious	*scared*	*overwhelmed*	*unburdened*
relieved	*determined*	*ready*	*able*
energized	*sad*	*orphaned*	*left out*
convinced	*hurt*	*self-protective*	*rejected*
paralyzed	*unsure*	*guilty*	*ashamed*
conflicted	*strong*	*self-reliant*	*supported*
desperate	*burdened*	*depressed*	*hopeless*
defeated	*disconsolate*	*confident*	*inspired*
	empowered	*liberated*	

_____ _____ _____ _____

_____ _____ _____ _____

_____ _____ _____ _____

_____ _____ _____ _____

◈   ◈   ◈

Journaling Exercise #43

Using at least six words from the catchphrase exercise, explore what you feel and why.

I feel _____ *because* _____

_____

_____

I feel _____ *because* _____

_____

_____

I feel _____ *because* _____

_____

_____

I feel _____ *because* _____

_____

_____

I feel _____ *because* _____

_____

_____

I feel _____ *because* _____

_____

_____

I feel _____ *because* _____

_____

_____

CONFRONTING THE CORE CONFLICT

Thinking/Journaling Exercise #44

Each of us has to come to terms with what I call *the core conflict*, the daughter's continuing need for maternal love and support versus her growing recognition of the damage the relationship causes. This exercise is in two parts. First, spend time thinking about where you locate yourself in the conflict at this moment—still engaged in it, beginning to extricate yourself from it, ready to move on from it—and using a free-flow style, write about it.

◈　　◈　　◈

Answer the following questions after using if/then thinking to come up with a plan:

What part of the conflict do I find hardest? Needing her love or honoring myself?

_____

_____

_____

_____

_____

*What strategies can I adopt to deal with the core conflict better?*_____

_____

_____

_____

_____

_____

Do I think the conflict can be resolved if I start honoring my own needs? Answer in detail.

_____

_____

_____

_____

_____

◈   ◈   ◈

FOCUSING ON SOLUTIONS

Journaling Exercise #45

In order to move forward and decide how you will manage your relationship with your mother going forward, you need as much emotional and mental clarity as possible.

Answer the following questions as honestly and fully as you can.

How much cultural or social pressure do I feel to continue the relationship? _____

_____

_____

_____

_____

_____

What are my greatest fears or worries about my decision? _____

_____

_____

_____

_____

_____

What are the primary obstacles to salvaging the relationship? _____

_____

_____

_____

_____

_____

Can I initiate a discussion with my mother? If not, why?

_____

_____

_____

_____

What rules or boundaries would have to be respected for the relationship to continue?

_____

_____

_____

_____

Is low or infrequent contact an option? Why or why not? _____

_____

_____

_____

How do I feel about going no-contact? _____

_____

_____

_____

_____

If I were to divorce my mother, what would happen?

_____

_____

_____

_____

_____

_____

_____

◈   ◈   ◈

IF YOU'VE GONE NO-CONTACT

Thinking/Journaling Exercise #46

Going no-contact sounds as though it's a single step but like everything else on this journey, it's really a process. Spend some time thinking about how you've acclimated emotionally to your decision and then answer the following questions.

Do I have any regrets about how I handled the situation looking back? _____

_____

_____

_____

_____

_____

_____

Are there moments that I doubt my choice? If so, what do I really question? _____

_____

_____

_____

_____

_____

Should I think about reestablishing contact? If so, why? _____

_____

_____

_____

_____

What about my own emotions and reactions has surprised me the most? _____

_____

_____

_____

_____

The hardest parts of going no-contact have been _____

_____

_____

_____

_____

RELATIONSHIP GOALS

Thinking/Journaling Exercise #47

Redirecting your life includes becoming a better gardener of what feeds your spirit, and relationships play a key role. It may be time to prune or cut back on some connections and move others into direct sun. Spend time thinking about five relational goals you want to set. They can be general (get out more, make new friends, develop a support system) or specific (better communicate my needs to my partner, stop getting angry when I'm threatened, give up a particular friendship that is more toxic than not). For each goal, come up with specific plans to achieve it.

Goal #1: _____

_____

_____

_____

_____

Goal #2: _____

_____

_____

_____

_____

Goal #3: _____

_____

_____

_____

_____

Goal #4: _____

_____

_____

_____

_____

       Goal #5: _____

_____

_____

_____

_____

◈   ◈   ◈

SELF-REFLECTION

Thinking/Journaling Exercise #48

This exercise asks you to examine how you define yourself. Studies show that people with a more complex definition of self are more resilient than those who define themselves primarily by one or two roles. Seeing the way you are self-limiting permits you to think about new directions. This exercise has two parts.

Part One: Spend time thinking about how you define yourself; you can focus on roles you play (spouse, friend, neighbor, mother, coworker, sibling, cousin, lawyer, sales assistant, etc.), activities that are central to your sense of self (lifelong learner, cook, gardener, confidante, tennis player, traveler, etc.), or both. Name at least six self-defining roles and activities and then elaborate on **(a)** why they are important to who you think you are and **(b)** how they sustain both in good times and stressful ones.

       I am _____

*(a)*_____

_____

*(b)*_____

_____

       I am _____

*(a)*_____

_(b)_ _____

_____

_I am_ _____

_(a)_ _____

_____

_(b)_ _____

_____

_I am_ _____

_(a)_ _____

_____

_(b)_ _____

_____

_I am_ _____

_(a)_ _____

_____

_(b)_ _____

_____

_I am_ _____

_(a)_ _____

_____

_(b)_ _____

_____

Part Two: Spend some time thinking about how you want to redefine yourself in the months and years ahead. Choose four new roles or activities that you believe might become central to your new sense of self and name them in the spaces below and elaborate on how you will achieve them and what you think they will change about how you define yourself.

I will be _____

_____

_____

_____

_____

I will be _____

_____

_____

_____

_____

I will be _____

_____

_____

_____

_____

I will be _____

_____

_____

_____

_____

SELF-COMPASSION

Visualization Exercise #4

We have to become better cheerleaders and emotional managers to redirect our lives. We have to fill the holes in our hearts with countermanding actions. We have to self-mother so that when we encounter a glitch or setback, we don't fall into old patterns. Do this exercise in a place where you feel comfortable and safe.

**Imagine yourself talking to the little girl you were
and encourage her to move forward.
Talk to her the way you always longed to be talked to.
Imagine that the two of you are on a long walk together, somewhere beautiful.
Open your heart to her.**

SELF-MOTHERING IN ACTION

Thinking/Journaling Exercise #49

Without your mother having a full-blown epiphany, working with you, and effecting a sincere reconciliation, none of the *"solutions"* for dealing with her and your family of origin are solutions in the traditional sense (and that hopeful scenario is very unlikely). Staying consciously aware of your emotions, especially your ambivalence, is key to the process. Each of the following questions or statements explores a negative internalized response. Elaborate on it, and then detail how you will work to mute it.

Do I sometimes still feel as though I am to blame? Explain. _____

_____

_____

_____

But I also know that I'm not at fault because _____

_____

_____

_____

What does your critical voice taunt you with? Explain.

_____

_____

_____

_____

I shut off the voice by saying this out loud: _____

_____

_____

_____

When I doubt myself, I feel _____

_____

_____

But then I am able to self-correct by realizing _____

_____

_____

_____

◈   ◈   ◈

REACTIVITY RECHECK

Thinking/Journaling Exercise #50

Spend some time thinking about how successful or unsuccessful you've been at disarming triggers, staying out of the self-criticism trap, paying attention to how you may be rejection-sensitive, and substituting approach for avoidance if you're fearful of failure. Do not take this as an opportunity to beat yourself up; use cool processing and a third-person perspective.

First, list three instances of positive progress, and explain why they're important.

Now, list three instances where you missed the mark and detail what you need to work on.

_____

_____

_____

_____

_____

_____

_____

_____

_____

_____

_____

_____

_____

_____

_____

MOTHERHOOD AS A CHOICE

Thinking/Journaling Exercise #51

Whether you are already a parent, still debating the question, or have already decided that you'll sit this one out, being consciously aware of your thinking and motivation is very important because this decision is a big one for those who've had painful childhood experiences. Answer the following questions as fully as you can with as much depth as possible.

Do I feel cultural pressure to have a child? _____

_____

_____

_____

Am I worried about repeating my mother's behaviors? _____

_____

_____

_____

What are my greatest concerns about the choice? _____

_____

_____

_____

In what ways would choosing to be a mother or deciding not to be one define me? _____

_____

_____

_____

EIGHT INSPIRATIONS

Thinking/Catchphrase Exercise #22

Come up with eight phrases, words, or sentences that you hope will define you and your life in the months and years ahead as you continue to redirect your life and move away from the old, inherited patterns of reacting and behaving. Some examples might be *"Feeling confident," "Being challenged and loving it," "Experiencing tranquility," "Being in balance," "Joyous," "Grateful for being me."*

Spend time thinking about the catchphrases and write them down. Chose four and expand upon them as fully as you can.

1. _____

_____

2. _____

_____

3. _____

_____

4. _____

_____

5. _____

_____

6. _____

_____

7. _____

_____

8. _____

_____

RECOVER

It's at this stage of the journey that we consider ourselves works in progress but getting closer to being healed and free from our childhood experiences. It's now that we must adjust our thinking about what it means to be healed, and recognize that the wholeness we will achieve is special and different. Drawing on the ancient Japanese art of *kintsugi* as the primary metaphor, we can embrace our transformation and begin to see the past from a different perspective. Our remaining reactivity is further diminished by the ability to manage and name our emotions, and our ability to navigate the world of relationships considerably enhanced.

In contrast to Western cultures where damage to objects of value—a painting, sculpture, or piece of glassware or china—is carefully hidden so that the objects appear never to have been broken in the first place, *kintsugi* takes a decidedly different approach. Using lacquer infused with the dust of precious metals such as gold, silver, and copper to fill in the breaks restores the piece but also emphasizes its history of damage as part of its wholeness. That can be true for unloved daughters as well.

Letting go of the toxicity and pain is key to recovery so we'll embark on a series of perspective-altering exercises to change our point of view, abandoning the sightlines we developed as children whose emotional needs weren't met. We focus on the importance of self-love, admiration, and compassion so that we can step into the breach left by childhood neglect and fill it with true caring. Most importantly, we learn to mother ourselves as we needed to be mothered. That leaves us whole when we are with friends and partners, no longer animated by neediness, and we're able to move toward earned security.

Mourning the mother we deserved and didn't get is an essential part of letting go and being on the road to the best possible version of ourselves we can imagine. Seeing that what we needed (and even craved) in childhood was normal and ordinary—it's what every child wants and needs—allows us to shuck that feeling of being the eternal outsider, that overly sensitive person who can't get a joke and is always complaining about something. Being able to grieve permits us to move to a place of acceptance that is full of clarity and devoid of denial or excuses and loosens the grip of the past on our hearts and psyches and lets us move freely and even gracefully into a future of our own making. Mourning allows you to recognize once and for all that nothing that happened had anything to do with you at all or who you were but everything to do with other people.

WHAT IS HEALING?

Thinking/Journaling Exercise #52

Your own thoughts about what it means to heal can either support or undermine your continued progress. Becoming conscious of what you feel and think deep-down is all-important. Answer as honestly as you can after engaging in reflection.

How do I define "healing"? What do I expect to experience? _____

_____

_____

_____

_____

*Do I see myself as "damaged" or "broken"? Please explain in detail.*_____

_____

_____

_____

_____

Does thinking about healing make you feel hopeful or anxious? Explain why. _____

_____

_____

_____

_____

Do you believe that you can heal sufficiently to recover from your childhood? _____

_____

_____

_____

Have you sought support for the process of healing? Comment on why, if you have or haven't.

_____

_____

_____

_____

_____

_____

_____

IMAGINING HEALING

Visualization/Catchphrase Exercise #5

Do this work when you have time and space and aren't in a rush. Put your cell phone where you can't hear it. Sit or lie down somewhere you can really focus on your body.

Ask yourself where you feel/store your emotional pain.
Does your throat or chest get tight or does it feel like a band around your head?
Is it a punch in the gut or a dull ache?
Visualize the place you feel your emotions first and breathe deep.
Focus in on it.
Now visualize a coursing stream or a beam of sunlight breaking through clouds.
Concentrate both on your body and that image of openness,
taking deeper and slower breaths as you close your eyes.
Imagine the pain being swept away by water,
the hidden hurt being brought into the light,
and continue to breathe deeply and relax into the moment.
Continue to sit or lie there quietly for another five to ten minutes.

When you are done, write down whatever comes into your mind about healing, and the parts of your body where you feel and store pain, below. Do this exercise as often as you need. If it doesn't work for you the first time, it's probably because you're too tense or armored; simply try it again. It's not a test.

_____

_____

_____

_____

_____

_____

_____

_____

_____

_____

◇　◇　◇

SETTING GOALS FOR HEALING

Thinking/Journaling Exercise #53

Recovery is a process, not a single step, and an important aspect of it is dealing with and managing the emotional pain of being unloved, which can persist long into adulthood—sometimes decades of adult life—and, counterintuitively, even after your mother's death. The brain circuitry for emotional and physical pain is one and the same, which explains a lot. Becoming proactive about your emotional skill set will help push you in the right direction. This is, once again, the mantra of conscious awareness. This exercise is in three parts. The first two parts can be done on the same day, but wait another day before completing the third part.

Part One: Identify four interactions or situations that continue to activate the feelings of sadness and pain associated with your childhood. These could be holidays or birthdays, specific situations you find stressful or challenging (meeting new people, going to a party, or anything else), or simply having a disagreement with someone. Use cool processing while thinking and writing about these moments, asking *why* you felt as you did and not *what* you felt.

Interaction/Situation: _____

_____

_____

_____

_____

Interaction/Situation: _____

_____

_____

_____

_____

Interaction/Situation: _____

_____

_____

_____

_____

Interaction/Situation: _____

_____

_____

_____

_____

Part Two: Work at identifying and naming the precise emotions you felt in the moment. Focus especially on blended emotions—such as feeling hurt but also angry, shamed but also bitter, etc. Write the emotions down and then explore why you felt as you did. (*"I felt hurt by what he said because it demeaned me and made me feel powerless as I did as a child. I ended up responding as if I were talking to my mother"; "I felt shunned and ashamed that I had no family at Christmas and became closed off and depressed, echoing old feelings."*)

I felt _____

because _____

_____

_____

I felt _____

because _____

_____

_____

I felt _____

because _____

_____

_____

I felt _____

because _____

_____

_____

Part Three: Do this at least a day after the others. Spend time thinking and then write about the strategies you'll use in the future to handle these situations and the triggering better.

To deal better with _____ ,

I will _____

_____

_____

To deal better with _____ ,

I will _____

_____

_____

To deal better with _____ ,

I will _____

_____

_____

To deal better with _____ ,

I will _____

_____

_____

◈   ◈   ◈

PROGRESS REPORT

Thinking/Journaling Exercise #54

It can be hard to be objective about the progress you're making, especially if you tend to be self-critical, so it can be helpful to play the roles of both teacher and student and write yourself a progress report. Keeping a record of all those baby steps and seeing how they end up being strides is not only cheerleading but also inculcates realism about the perseverance this journey requires. So, it's a win-win. Pick one skill you're working on—not ruminating, cutting down on reactivity, managing a specific negative emotion, being more approach-oriented, etc.—and make notes on your progress every month for the next six months in the slots below. Date them. If you want, you can use a notebook or extra pieces of paper to keep a progress chart of other skills as well.

I'm working on _____ *Date started* _____

Progress for Month 1: _____

_____

_____

_____

_____

Progress for Month 2: _____

_____

_____

_____

_____

Progress for Month 3: _____

_____

_____

_____

_____

_____

Progress for Month 4: _____

_____

_____

_____

Progress for Month 5: _____

_____

_____

_____

Progress for Month 6: _____

_____

_____

_____

◈   ◈   ◈

VISUALIZING THE MOTHER YOU DESERVED

Visualization/Journaling Exercise #6

Recognizing that you are worthy of love, support, and attention—and that you always were—can continue to be difficult for some daughters, which is what this two-part exercise is intended to combat. The first part is a pure visualization; the second is an expanded journal entry.

Part One: Visualization

Do this exercise when you are feeling calm, and not stressed, in a place you are comfortable. Use cool processing.

Begin by looking at either a childhood or adolescent photo of yourself,
remembering what that girl was like—
what made her laugh and what made her cry,
what she most loved to do, the stories she held close to her heart,
what she dreamed about, how she felt about herself.
She can be any age you like.

Now, close your eyes and imagine her with the mother she deserved.
You can draw on images of women you wished were your mother
to make the visualization more vivid.

Imagine the two of you just talking on a park bench,
or taking a stroll through a garden, chatting as you go.
Or walking along the banks of a river or on the beach,
talking about anything and everything, face to face.

Or perhaps you're little and she's having a tea party with you and your dolls,
or pushing you on a swing in the park, or coloring with you.
Visualize her listening to you intently and focus in on how that makes you feel.

When you open your eyes, realize that in a fair world,
your needs would have been met just the way you imagined.

Do this exercise as often as needed to bolster your belief in yourself and your perceptions.

Part Two: Writing the Mother You Deserved and Needed

Writing about the mother you deserved not only undermines the false notions that there was something wrong with you or that you somehow deserved your mother's treatment but also helps you realize that what you wanted and didn't get was both legitimate and normal. Really believing that your needs were both legitimate and unmet is key to recovery.

Think first and then make your answers as detailed and vivid as possible.

When she'd see me, she would _____

_____

_____

_____

_____

_____

If I were in need of comfort, distressed, or scared, she would _____

_____

_____

_____

_____

_____

If I succeeded at something, she'd respond by _____

_____

_____

_____

_____

_____

Things she would never do _____

_____

_____

_____

_____

Things she would always do _____

_____

_____

_____

_____

What I missed most and what affected me most by not having a mother like her _____

_____

_____

_____

_____

_____

_____

_____

MOURNING THE MOTHER YOU DESERVED

Journaling Exercise #55

Elizabeth Kübler-Ross and David Kessler lay out the five stages of grief through which a person who's experienced loss passes in their book *On Grief and Grieving*. These five stages apply to the unloved daughter's journey, too, as you recognize your pain, acknowledge your losses, and begin to mourn the mother you deserved—the one who listened to you, knew you, engaged in dialogue with you, apologized for her mistakes and let you apologize for yours, and loved you. Refer to Chapter Nine in *Daughter Detox* for more detail. Following are the five stages; please describe your own experiences as you moved through them. If you have not yet experienced a stage, that's worth noting, too. While they are presented in their original order, Kübler-Ross and Kessler make it clear that they may not happen to you in this sequence.

Denial: _____

_____

_____

_____

Anger: _____

_____

_____

_____

Bargaining: _____

_____

_____

_____

Depression: _____

_____

_____

_____

_____

Acceptance: _____

_____

_____

_____

_____

◈　　◈　　◈

COLLECTING INSPIRATIONS

Journaling Exercise #56

Finding the right words to express yourself, especially feelings of great import such as loss, is often hard but collecting the words of others can bring both clarity and healing. You can write down your own words in the spaces below or those of others. One of my favorites is by Lao Tzu: *"The journey of a thousand miles begins with a single step."*

_____

_____

_____

_____

WORKING ON SELF-MOTHERING

Visualization/Catchphrase Exercise #7

One way of filling the hole in your heart is for you to become the mother you needed by loving and supporting yourself. Again, make time for this exercise and find a place where you can lie down comfortably and won't be disturbed. If visualization comes easily to you, you might not need physical prompts, but if it doesn't, hold something fragile in your hand; it could be an egg, something delicate that is easily broken or torn, or even a cut flower. You'll notice that your hand has to be relaxed and slightly cupped, not clenched, which is the state of mind we're aiming for. If you're proceeding without a prompt, bring to mind a very small baby; it could be human, a kitten, puppy, or a nestling.

Now, imagine that it's your job
to keep what's fragile and helpless out of wind and rain,
and safe in every sense of the word.
Close your eyes and imagine
that what you are guarding and protecting is *you*
and everything about *you* that's unique and lovable.
Imagine yourself in the softest of featherbeds,
encircled by your arms or those of someone
who makes you feel safe in the world,
with the sounds of rustling leaves or lapping waves.

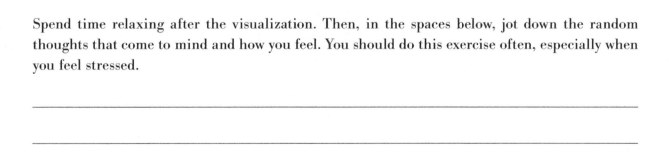

Spend time relaxing after the visualization. Then, in the spaces below, jot down the random thoughts that come to mind and how you feel. You should do this exercise often, especially when you feel stressed.

_____

_____

_____

_____

_____

_____

_____

_____

◈   ◈   ◈

SHIFTING PERSPECTIVE

Thinking/Journaling Exercise #57

While much of the work of *Daughter Detox* has us discover, discern, disarm, and reclaim by focusing on what we missed and how our emotional needs weren't met, a counterintuitive part of recovery requires a shift in perspective: what our mothers missed out on.

Think broadly about what she never understood about you or what she never witnessed because she was too self-involved or couldn't be bothered—your talents and gifts, your personality, the people in your life, your achievements and milestones. This is another way of drawing your own self-portrait as distinct from the child, girl, or woman your mother thought she saw.

What she didn't/doesn't know about me: _____

_____

_____

_____

_____

My mother never noticed _____

_____

_____

_____

_____

She missed out on _____

_____

_____

_____

_____

Moments and milestones she ignored _____

_____

_____

_____

_____

_____

Why she lost out _____

_____

_____

_____

_____

_____

_____

_____

THE QUESTION OF FORGIVENESS

Thinking/Journaling Exercise #58

There's often social, cultural, and sometimes religious pressure on a daughter to forgive her mother's behavior, whether she's in contact with her or has low or no contact. She may feel terrible about herself for not *"doing the right thing"* and forgiving. But forgiveness remains a complex and thorny issue for many and there's really no one right answer. This exercise is meant only to clarify your own thinking, not to push you in one direction or another.

Do you personally believe forgiveness is necessary? _____

_____

_____

_____

_____

_____

How does or doesn't it apply to your situation with your mother? _____

_____

_____

_____

_____

_____

Has forgiveness played a role in other relationships? Explain. _____

_____

_____

_____

_____

Have you tried forgiving your mother? Has it worked?

_____

_____

_____

_____

_____

_____

Further thoughts you might have: _____

_____

_____

_____

_____

_____

_____

◈   ◈   ◈

EARNED SECURITY

Visualization Exercise #8

In addition to working on shutting down the old triggers and making sure that you are reacting in the present, you can try to strengthen your ability to act as a securely attached woman does—believing in her own self-worth, wanting and cultivating healthy emotional connections, being open to new experiences, and trusting in the validity of her own perceptions—through visualization. If you want, you can use photographs of people you care about with whom you've felt safe and seen, as well as images of experiences you shared together, as prompts and inspiration.

Sit or lie down somewhere comfortable and close your eyes,
bringing to mind what some experts have called *"islands,"*
safe relationships that contrasted sharply
with how you were treated at home, remembering how you felt in detail.
These might have been times with a loving aunt or other relative,
a neighbor or someone else's parent,
a teacher, a pastor, or a friend,
or anyone who came into your life at any point;
it could even be your spouse or lover.
Explore those moments as you would a beautiful island,
taking in the magic,
and allow yourself to trust and be open.

WORKING ON EARNED SECURITY

Thinking/Journaling Exercise #59

Identify the people in your life with whom you find yourself interacting in new and more secure ways; think about them as the "islands" in your present life. Choose one or two people and, in the spaces below, think about and comment on why they bring out the best in you and what your "best self" looks like.

I am most myself and least reactive when I am with someone who is _____

_____

_____

_____

_____

_____

_____

I think I do best when I am around people who consistently _____

_____

_____

_____

I find myself at my most open when I feel _____

_____

_____

_____

The behaviors I still need to work on and pay attention to are _____

_____

_____

_____

What I have learned about relationships and connection that I didn't know or realize

before _____

_____

_____

_____

_____

REVISITING THE CORE CONFLICT

Thinking/Journaling Exercise #60

It's the core conflict that keeps us emotionally connected to our mothers, no matter how toxic and damaging the relationship, makes us doubt ourselves, and amps up our emotional neediness. Locate where you find yourself emotionally in the battle and then answer the following questions.

How close am I to resolving the conflict? _____

_____

_____

_____

_____

What, if anything, is the greatest impediment to my healing? _____

_____

_____

_____

_____

_____

What am I still hanging on to that I must learn to let go of? _____

_____

_____

_____

_____

What active steps can I take to further promote my healing?

_____

_____

_____

_____

_____

_____

◈   ◈   ◈

THE ROAD AHEAD

Visualization Exercise #9

Before you do this exercise, revisit the self-calming exercise on pages 57-58.

Visualize a situation that would have formerly pushed all of your buttons.
It could be an argument with someone,
the moment after you feel someone has put you down or mocked you,
going into a room full of strangers,
or any other setting that is potentially stressing.

See yourself as you would optimally handle the situation,
first defusing all of your automatic emotional responses
and then acting in full consciousness.

Imagine yourself behaving as your very best self,
demonstrating your newfound strength and ability to
articulate what you're feeling and being able to act as you wish to.

STRATEGIES GOING FORWARD

Thinking/Journaling Exercise #61

Focusing on the short-term—let's say the next two or three months—think about and then journal about the strategies you will implement to promote your continued movement forward. These could include avoidant strategies—such as staying out of situations which will unnecessarily stress you out—as well as proactive strategies which will get you out into the world more and expand your horizons, such as traveling or trying something new.

Until I'm ready, the kinds of situations I still need to be wary of are _____

_____

_____

_____

Should an altercation or disagreement arise with someone, my strategy will be to _____

_____

_____

_____

I will use STOP, LOOK, LISTEN and self-talk when _____

_____

_____

_____

Techniques I will use to disarm my reactivity under stress are _____

_____

_____

_____

SETTING LONG-TERM GOALS

Thinking/Journaling Exercise #62

Where do you want to find yourself one year from now? In three? Or in five? Think about the goals you want to set for yourself in every aspect of your life and set the bar according to what you have learned about yourself. Forgo pie-in-the-sky thinking for if/then strategies. Try to be *both* optimistic and clear headed.

One year from now, I see myself _____

_____

_____

_____

_____

In three years, I hope to _____

_____

_____

_____

_____

My goals for my life five years from now are _____

_____

_____

_____

_____

A Letter to My Younger Self

Journaling Exercise #63

Write a letter to your younger self—you can pick any age from childhood to young adulthood—and talk to her about what you know now and she didn't then.

My dear .... ,

SEEING MYSELF ANEW

Self-Portrait Exercise

Use these pages to create a self-portrait of yourself as you see yourself now. You can make this as literal as you wish—by pasting a photograph on the page or, if you're inclined, drawing a self-portrait—or as abstract as you wish.

You can also use words to "paint" your self-portrait, either written by hand or typed up and then cut and pasted. The words could reflect your activities and hobbies (gardener, tennis player), roles you play (mother, neighbor, confidante), your strengths (good listener, compassionate), or even your goals and dreams (world traveler, aspiring chef).

Alternatively, you can use photographic images, either cut from magazines or downloaded and printed, to symbolize how you see yourself now. Or, if you like, you can create a portrait of yourself as you will be next year or the year after, using the same techniques.

Spend time thinking about the qualities that make you unique before you begin.

MUSINGS ON THE SELF

Thinking/Journaling Exercise #64

Before you begin to write, think about whether your self-portrait represents qualities you have always had, but were unable to see, because of the habit of self-criticism, or whether some of these are new and part of emotional and psychological growth.

What aspects of yourself were you most blind to and why? _____

_____

_____

What has surprised you most about the ways you've been able to reclaim yourself? _____

_____

_____

_____

In what ways do you see your life getting better as you progress? _____

_____

_____

_____

What do you know now about yourself that you didn't before? _____

_____

_____

_____

What's the most important piece of advice you'd give yourself at this juncture? _____

_____

_____

_____

NOTES ON THE JOURNEY

Thinking/Journaling Exercise #65

Spend time thinking about the nature of this journey, reflecting on both the losses and the triumphs and the changes in yourself you have witnessed. Make note of what surprised, thrilled, and even dismayed you. This space is yours to use as you see fit.

Godspeed!

_____

_____

_____

_____

_____

_____

_____

_____

_____

_____

_____

_____

_____

_____

_____

_____

_____

◈　　◈　　◈

SUBJECT INDEX TO EXERCISES

The exercises in the book are progressive and are meant to be done in sequence the first time. But after you've completed the workbook, you may find it useful to return to certain exercises to build up specific skills, to refocus or further clarify your thinking, or to revisit a topic in depth. You may also want to do some of the journaling exercises more than once in a separate notebook.